Second Act Entrepreneur

by Eric Brown

First published in July 2021

Edited and formatted by Sean Donovan.

ISBN: 9798536923641
Imprint: Independently published

Printed in the United States of America.

Contents

Synopsis

This book of marketing and branding musings was created to help push folks — those sitting on the fence and paralyzed with fear — into the world of entrepreneurship. According to author Eric Brown, "...for every job that has vanished there are 10 new opportunities." *From Apartments to Hot Sauce* recounts Eric's journey as an entrepreneur and was written for those would-be entrepreneurs who are stuck in the middle — caught between one career and the next, with a great idea and some business experience, but uncertain about how to get traction for their idea.

The book includes fascinating stories of how Eric marketed a boutique apartment business in Detroit, Michigan and how he grew his hot sauce business using many of the same techniques... and how it led to a 10,000-unit real estate portfolio across the southwest. This book tackles the fear that accompanies an entrepreneur's leap of faith, as well as learning how to shift gears as conditions dictate, and managing scalability and growth.

Prologue

The gap between the haves and the have-nots continues to widen, so they say. The middle class has evaporated; or is it just wrapped differently? I feel for folks who are out of work, as some jobs may never return; however, for every job that has vanished, ten more opportunities have popped up.

This book is for the folks in the middle, maybe between one career and the next, who possess a great idea and business experience, but are wondering how to get traction for their idea. Although many of the examples are about how we marketed our boutique apartment business, Urbane Apartments, in Detroit MI, and subsequently our hot sauce business in Hamtramck, MI, and then scaled those ideas to market and brand a 10,000-unit portfolio than spans across Arizona, Texas and Oklahoma, it is really about my path; doing one thing for twenty-five years, then changing direction and doing something else. Reinvent is an overused term, but sometimes it applies—and sometimes doing it sooner than later is beneficial. There is no better time than now.

This book is also about overcoming fear and mustering up the courage to do something different. I also cover scaling your idea, which was perhaps the hardest piece of all. But mostly, it is just my story, and I hope you find a nugget or two that helps you along and allows you to get out of your own way and enjoy the journey.

Back to the middle class, has it really evaporated, or have we just lost our way? Growing up on a farm in mid-state Ohio, life was a bit different in comparison to now. Actually, it was very different. My father was a homebuilder and a part-time farmer. I could gauge what type of year my dad was having with his business based on the car we were driving. In a good year, he was sporting a new Cadillac and a new Ford pick-up truck, but in those inevitable down years, we drove an Impala and had no new trucks. For sure, we had less stuff then, opposed to now. We had one TV, one car, and one phone. We rarely dined out. There was no cable TV, we had an antenna and a rotor.

Today there is a TV in every bedroom, plus a cell phone for every family member, plus a laptop for every family member, plus an iPad for every family member. We have cable TV with movie channels, and internet service in multiple places; on our phones, in the house, on our iPads, and on our WIFI. Yep, the world is a bit fuller, and somewhat more complicated; or is it?

Branding and marketing on a budget is as important as ever. You need to be able to sell; yourself and your product or idea. Selling is easier with a sprinkle of solid branding and marketing.

Many small business proprietors who ramble on and on about customer service and quality in order to justify their pricing are missing a very important point; it's not about the money. Impeccable customer service and quality are the starting point, certainly a must-do. To sustain charging a greater price than your competitor, your brand must establish and behave in a manner that is remarkable.

Remarkable, as defined by the legend Seth Godin:

- "Remarkable doesn't mean remarkable to you. It means remarkable to me. Am I going to make a remark about it?
- 'Being noticed is not the same as being remarkable. Running down the street naked will get you noticed, but it won't accomplish much. It's easy to pull off a stunt, but not useful."

Is the experience you are creating for your customer remarkable, and does your customer find value in the experience created? Are you matching your brand to a targeted experience?

Service excellence, just as with beauty, is in the eye of the beholder.

Take some time to evaluate what will engage and delight your customer, based on your brand. Stop in at the local Mini Cooper dealership and you'll notice they openly invite customers to bring their beloved pets into the dealership, which some folks get really excited about. It works for Mini Cooper, but you likely would not find that at the Jaguar showroom. Mini Cooper is matching a customer experience to their brand. This example has no correlation to luxury and doesn't get better by adding more money. Southwest Airlines, you either love them or hate them, with their cattle-call lines, no assigned seats, and no frills. Yet true Southwest customers *like, enjoy, laugh with, and have a favorable experience with Southwest*. Herb Kelleher, Southwest co-founder, somehow figured out how to deliver a consistent, value-driven experience and he permitted his employees to fix it when it wasn't.

With our boutique apartment management company, Urbane Apartments in Royal Oak, MI, we have used some innovative ideas to create remarkable experiences for our residents that align with our brand. Our angle is, and has always been, "We aren't for everyone". We have never tried to be all things to all people. Generalists work on narrow, "lowest price gets the prize" margins. Boutique brands enjoy much wider margins and have a healthy air of snarky persona.

Sometimes it takes one of life's jolts to push us in this or that direction. That is how I figured out how to market and brand our businesses, because I had to. Although I had no formal training, schooling, or marketing degrees, I have been forever fascinated with why consumers buy this versus that, and the varying price points between somewhat, or mostly, similar products.

I am not always the easiest cat in town to deal with. I've been fired as a client more than once. I'm not very proud of that, but it is what it is. When it happened with the marketing studio that was doing our marketing and PR work, I was taken aback. The timing was really bad, or at least it seemed so. We were getting ready to launch a marketing campaign for the biggest deal I had ever attempted to develop. I had a lot of risk and exposure with the development. I have, irrespective of the climate pressures, never, ever been afraid to question things. This is the point here, and neither should you, even at the risk of being fired.

As it turned out, that was a pinnacle point in our business, and my growth as an entrepreneur. We started to figure out content marketing way before it was popular, as we developed our digital footprint. When we started to self-generate leasing leads to rent apartments with no traditional advertising, people started to notice.

Chapter 1
Do You Know Where You Are Going?

What was about to unfold would alter the direction of my life. That sounds a bit dramatic, but most of us spend very little time intentionally thinking about the direction of our lives. It's almost like we just let the winds of our habits propel us through our day; until we get that jolt, then suddenly, we are traversing an entirely different path.

So, on that day many years ago, I mindlessly headed to the drugstore that my dad had built for my uncle. Although brothers, my dad and uncle had very different personalities. Both were successful business guys, at least up to that point. My uncle was a pharmacist, and my dad was a contractor. They really were my earliest examples of entrepreneurs, except back then, I am not sure I knew what an entrepreneur was. Looking back, nobody in my family worked for anyone else. They all had different businesses. Both my dad and my uncle had been self-employed for as long as I could remember, and they owned a lot of businesses in our small town.

I happened to see my dad that morning in the parking lot and, out of the blue, he tells me he has been having an affair. He then proceeds to tell me he was leaving our small Ohio town, headed for

Florida. I knew things weren't going well with some of his businesses, and that he owed the bank a lot of money. His trucks and construction equipment were sold, and the bank took back unsold spec houses and building lots. Most of the other businesses that he had started closed up as well. He crumbled. Looking back, he could have worked his way through it, but he didn't. I have only seen my dad a few times since that strange day. What unfolded after that floored me, and in a nano-second, my dreams of taking over his construction business evaporated.

That day was my first look at the good, the bad, and the ugly of running a business. Little did I know, at the time, just how much this radical shift in my life's direction affected me. Thinking back, it may have been more of my dad's dream for me to be involved in his business than my own.

Dad was a homebuilder and a part-time farmer on our 60-acre farm in Ohio. I guess my first lesson in economics was realizing that the year, make and model of the vehicle(s) in our driveway was a direct indication of the kind of year he was having financially. Although they were not overly frugal, my parents rarely lived beyond their means.

I learned many lessons on our family farm, but mostly I learned about hard work. Our farm wasn't necessarily a real farm; it was more of a hobby for my workaholic dad, but there was always something to do. I had a rigid set of chores that consisted of watering and feeding the animals, chopping ice out of the frozen water tanks in the winter, and cutting lots and lots of grass in the summer.

My dad and grandfather farmed some of the land, mostly at night after Dad was already done with a full day's work. They bailed hay a lot, which made me sneeze, and that seemed like pretty hard work. As a kid, I followed behind the tractor and plow, watching the turning of the earth as Dad drove.

My last memory of cutting grass on the farm was running over some sticks with the new mower and trying to get them out before they dulled the blades. My dad was pretty strict and had laid down the law and put the fear of God in me about running over sticks and trying to pull them out. My effort proved unsuccessful. The binding pulled my hand under the mower and whacked off one of my fingertips! Luckily, I found it and my mom rushed me to the ER. Life on the farm wasn't really for me.

The space on the farm worked well for Dad's construction business. There was plenty of room to park the trucks and equipment as his remodeling and new home construction business grew. By the time I was a sophomore in high school, I was working 40 hours a week after school in a program in which I went to school from 8am to 11am and then worked afterward. My dad wasn't big on formal education, rather learning and honing a trade was much more important than a traditional college education to him. So, I learned to be a mason, carpenter, painter and so on. My dad always said, "If you can make a living with your hands, no one can ever take that away from you."

By the early 1980s, my dad owned several businesses—a sizable construction company, a paint store, a carpet shop, a bar and restaurant, and a beauty shop. He owned a lot of land in our small hometown, and he had a vision that I was going to come into the business. He even changed the name of the construction business to include '& Son.' I was still in school, and I thought that was cool.

After my senior year, I worked a full year in his business, and I was married by the time I was 21. That is kind of what you did in our small town in mid-state Ohio. So, it seemed to make sense at the time. Little did I know I would grow restless and yearn to move on to bigger things. I should stress here, bigger, not necessarily better.

It was the 1980s; interest rates were skyrocketing to twenty-plus percent and Dad's businesses started to dissolve. Then, on that fateful day in the drugstore parking lot, I went from thinking I was going to be a business owner to being unemployed. At the same time, what Dad did not know when he left my life that day was that my wife, at the time, was pregnant with twins.

I couldn't spend any time thinking about him and his problems and what he did to my mom. I needed to think about finding a job to take care of my own growing family. Everyone I knew encouraged me to get a "real job". I had been doing construction-related side jobs along the way, but apparently those didn't qualify as "real jobs", at least in my wife's family. So, I applied at the only factory-type occupation around, the International Car Company of Kenton, Ohio. At that time, the company was a major player in caboose manufacturing, particularly from the 1960s to 1980s. By the 1970s, only a few railroads were still manufacturing their own cabooses, and most were turning to more standardized designs.

This company would have been perfect for me to land a carpenter position, where I would have crafted the woodwork on the caboose interiors. I got a job, but I wasn't crafting woodwork. Instead, I was hired as a sweep – which is exactly what it sounds like. I was supposed to be the one who swept up after everyone - and, as I was told from one of the other guys, that was all I would ever amount to.

Either way, on my first day, I worked pretty hard sweeping up. I assumed if I did a good job, when something opened up in the carpentry shop, I might get a chance. To my surprise, and confusion, I was also told that I needed to hide out and stop working that hard. "We don't work that hard around here," they said. I could not comprehend that kind of work ethic at any level, so while I am sure that was not how all factory jobs were run, my first impression was a bad one. I quickly figured out that factory work just wasn't in my blood, and I quit by day three. It also set a tone for me about union shop labor.

So, what happens when you just up and quit a new job with a pregnant wife who is expecting twins? You start your own business, of course. Looking back, being an entrepreneur was all I knew growing up, and my dad and my uncle were my first introduction to the concept. As I mentioned, I never remember a time when either of them was not self-employed. Although they never called themselves 'entrepreneurs', Dad did talk a lot about the importance of self-employment and small business. He used to say over and over, "If a man knows a trade, he will always be employed. Learning a craft is something that no one can ever take away from you." That served my dad well, as he was an excellent carpenter. For me, not so much, so I decided I wanted to manage the trades as opposed to work in them.

The same day that I left that factory job, I walked into the local Ford dealership and bought a brand-new truck; a trait I learned from Dad that would not serve me well. Instead of buying something new, I could have bought it used and paid cash. It would have worked just as well. New is fine IF you have the cash, except I didn't, so I borrowed the money. Borrowing money is okay for certain things, and inevitable in business, but I would soon learn that no one ever makes money by paying interest. Borrowed money will soon eat your lunch.

With my brand-new toolboxes and my Brown Construction sign in hand (much to my in-laws' chagrin), I was now in business. The only problem was that I didn't have any jobs lined up. Living in a small town has benefits for sure, but one drawback is that once something happens to you, everyone knows about it.

After Dad crashed his businesses and left with his mistress, it left my mom a bit embarrassed. Even still, the town and local business owners welcomed me warmly. They told me that I shouldn't worry about what Dad did and that I should just do my work, so I did. With a lot of hustle, I started to line up some jobs – a roofing job here, a siding job there – and after I finished each one, I put a sign out front that said, *"Another fine job by Brown Construction."*

Looking back, those signs were a valuable first business lesson that would serve me well later. Branding yourself and your business need not be expensive. It can be as simple as putting out a sign after a job well done. Even if we were only changing locksets at a property, we would put up a job sign and leave it up for as long as we could. Soon, our branded job signs were popping up all over the neighborhood, and more importantly, they were being talked about.

Getting people to talk about you and/or your brand or business is called word-of-mouth marketing. Soon, business was bursting at the seams, and I found myself working seven days a week to keep pace with demand. The job signs also helped us create a perception that we were bigger than we were. Perception is reality and, while we were a very small contractor in the beginning, it led to larger jobs and continued growth. Interestingly, a very similar outcome would occur again 20 years later with our Urbane Apartment business.

The only problem was that my lack of business experience was showing, and these larger jobs were costing me more than I was charging. I became intoxicated by the new business, mistaking expansion for profits. Sometimes it was a difference of a few thousand dollars, but as my business grew, it became a difference of hundreds of thousands of dollars. You see, when your business is growing and is bringing in more revenue each quarter than the previous quarter, coupled with the gurus telling you that business success is all about cash flow, your problems can be well masked. The faster I ran, the bigger hole I was digging.

Business success isn't all about cash flow; actually, that is only part of the truth. Increased cash flow can easily disguise a larger, looming problem. With increased revenue each month, we were able to pay off last month's bills with this month's income—at least for a while. That works as long as the size of your jobs get bigger each month and you continue to grow. It doesn't work so well if you want to stop, or your business growth slows. I just wasn't paying attention to the money, and it would soon catch up with me in a devastating way.

Unfortunately, what was happening with my business went way beyond my understanding at that time in my life. In hindsight, I should have gone back to my customers and told them that the amount I quoted them for the work was off, and it was going to cost more and then give them the reasons why. Most likely, they would have been okay with the change, but that isn't what I did. I was more worried about what they might think of me, or that they wouldn't like me, or that they might think I didn't know what I was doing (I really didn't). The truth is, what we think others think about us might have some truth to it, but it shouldn't define us. Often, we get sideways due to that little voice in our head.

Fear shows up for all of us in so many different ways. Instead of facing my fear, I tried to make up the losses on the next job, but the jobs got bigger and so did the mistakes. This led to my biggest mistake of all, which was that I did not pay the required payroll taxes on my employees. By the time I was 30, I racked up enough back taxes to the government to stifle even the bravest of souls. I learned early on that it is very easy to get into business, but it is much, much harder to get out. I also learned that selling is much easier than executing and, at that time, I was able to sell more than I could produce. The moral of this story is: selling is easy, execution is tough.

More Lessons Learned

My first roll of the entrepreneurial dice was the construction company that I started in my early 20s and crashed before I turned 30. It was a devastating blow. I followed in my father's footsteps and walked straight off the cliff. That experience created more emotional scars than anything; however, during this harrowing time in my life, I learned that I was resilient. Somehow, I figured out how to get the back taxes paid off over a few years by working for 'the man' in a regular job. While I got the financial burden off of my back, the emotional burden of shame was now even bigger.

Entrepreneurs fail to talk about the shame and embarrassment that choke holds you after a crash.

Once I filed bankruptcy, I moved away from that little town and got a regular job in another city. Before long, life was pretty good again. Money was flowing thanks to raises and advances, and I buried my shame deep within. It wouldn't be until years later that I would understand just how far I buried it. I realized the depths of my shame when we came back to my hometown on the weekends. Even 25 years later, I can barely go into my local, hometown grocery store because I'm embarrassed about what happened. That's how long an entrepreneur who failed can carry their shame.

Today I live in Detroit, where the news is dominated by what is going on in the auto industry. I remember when former GM leader, Rick Wagner, was speaking at a press conference, just after the first government loan discussion. He was revealing the company's woes. What struck me was his comment that the company had enough cash to remain solvent for only six weeks. How could a company that may have once been one of the best in America, maybe the best in the world, only have enough cash on hand for six weeks!?

Hearing Wagner admit this truth was actually an epiphany for me. It made me think about my dad's businesses some 30 years prior, but more importantly, it made me think about my own. I emerged from losing my construction business with a huge burden of inadequacy and the feeling that I couldn't manage money responsibly. Even though we covered payroll and got through it, sometimes the crazy little demons in your head take over and you freeze, wallowing in self-criticism.

Events we experience along life's pathway sometimes etch tracks in our head, and we replay those tapes repeatedly. We create habits around those tracks and, as the saying goes, "Our habits define us". Some are good habits and tracks, some not so much. One track that has stuck with me for over 40 years is 'running out of money', which is the common denominator I remember about both Dad's businesses and mine. We both ran out of money.

Fortunately, I proved myself wrong about my inability to handle money and, for the next 10 years, I worked for another company, rose to the top, and was able to manage money quite effectively. By this point, I looked successful, had money in the bank, and a BMW in the driveway. Life was good, sort of, if working for the man is your idea of fun. For me, something else was becoming more important—my time. I grew bored and wanted another roll of the dice; another chance to create wealth all on my own.

Returning to Business Ownership

Ironically, it was on Father's Day, while sitting on the porch and talking to my three older kids, that I made the decision to, once again, start my own business. When my oldest daughter, then in her 20s, asked me why I didn't take the chance, I brought up the shame of my past failure. I told her how I caused a bunch of chaos back then and how I didn't want to do that again. She reminded me that my shame took place 20 years ago and she told me that I didn't cause chaos. Her comments were a turning point for me. To my kids, my failure really wasn't that big of a deal. So why was it a big deal to me? Why couldn't I just let go of the baggage? Her comments were a real wakeup call for me.

Re-entering the ranks of self-employment wasn't without its obstacles. The Great Recession of 2008 took its toll on my business. A few years into our Urbane branded apartments and our boutique apartment management business start-up, I made a deal [insert bad deal] with a partner on an apartment community we acquired together. If you look in the dictionary, this partner's photo would be found under 'Pitbull.'

Halfway through our rehab of this apartment community, our lender announced that there would not be any more funding deals in Michigan. Um, notice a pattern here... running out of money.

"We are what we think about." This phrase will guide you through how to learn to pivot your thoughts in the following chapters and save you a bushel basket of troubles.

I learned another tough lesson about reading the fine print in loan documents because again, I fell deeply into debt. The bank stopped lending us the money even though we had a loan with them. We finished the project in 2008 in spite of negative cash flow. We had to get creative, but we got it done. It was a scary time, and I didn't sleep much at night during those low times between 2008 and 2010, but as my grandmother used to say, "This too shall pass," and it did. We became much better operators in those low times.

What struck me during those times was that often we really do not see the future all that well. Instead, we know that we are climbing, and we know when things aren't going well and we are in a freefall, but we don't seem to recognize the top or the bottom. It's important to watch and monitor your performance, and/or your metrics. These numbers can help to properly steer your efforts in your business and help you predict how calm or turbulent the future waters will be. This is important so you don't crash your boat on the rocks because you were blindsided by what you should have seen coming.

Still Learning

I learned that I would never do something again if it felt difficult or uneasy. This deal with the pitbull just didn't feel right from the start. I ignored my inner compass and pushed ahead anyway, but the sad thing is that our business was just about to crest. We had just about paid back the money from our start-up mistakes that inevitably happened. Then I went and filled the boat with water again. That deal, which happened in about year six of our business, almost brought us down completely. It took several years to recover.

I also learned to never do a deal without already having the money lined up. In 2008, Detroit was going through a god-awful time, but the people who sailed through it unscathed were sitting on a war chest of cash, not credit—cash. Up until this point, I had never lined the cash up first in my deals. I jumped and thought I could do without it, but the reality is that I needed money. While I believe in the "ready, fire, aim" approach, meaning you will not have all the answers before you start your business, ship your product, and so on, it is not responsible to ignore the money. Bootstrapping is an overused cliché.

Sidebar

Definition: What is bootstrapping? It is the act of starting a business with little or no money.

End Sidebar

Infomercials tout using OPM (Other People's Money), but when you take on an equity partner, they give you the money with conditions, of course. That means that the investor wants to know what type of return they will get on their capital and equity. In my experience, the reason we were able to grow our Urbane branded apartment business is because we had kick ass cash on cash returns. Another way to say this is, "You are only as good as your last deal." It is just like watching the people who are pitching on the television show Shark Tank. The first question they are asked is, "How much have you sold?"

I'm not the only one who jumped into a business deal with blinders on. Statistics show that in the first five years of business, 60 percent of entrepreneurs go under. In years five to ten, an even higher percentage go out of business. So, if you want to start a business and you are already sucking for air on day one because you used credit cards to fund your venture, it will only get harder as you go along. Add in those holes, sometimes craters, you create along the way that are riddled with mistakes, and it can be a rough go.

Perhaps the most important thing that I learned throughout all of this was that I thought this stuff just happened to me. After talking to other business folks and entrepreneurs, I discovered that things happen to all of us, and we need to learn how to deal with curveballs.

Looking back, all of the problems I experienced were solvable had I chosen to solve them. Even the failures of Dad's businesses and my construction business, so many years ago, were solvable, had I made that choice, except I didn't. The overarching point here is that there will be problems with your business, but if you stick your head in the sand, failure occurs. Choose to deal with challenges, and once you make that commitment, you have planted the metaphorical seeds of success.

At about year eight or nine, our Urbane Apartments business finally turned the corner, which means it was producing enough positive, consistent cash flow that our income outpaced our expenses. By about year ten, the business was producing enough consistent cash flow that, as Robert Kiyosaki touts in his series of *Rich Dad* books, I got off the hamster wheel.

Sidebar

Getting off the hamster wheel: When you keep running in circles and do not progress toward what you want.

End Sidebar

For me, getting off the hamster wheel meant finally being able to spend my time differently. I was finally able to do things and projects that matter to me, as opposed to always working the grind. Now, I am mostly just overseeing the business.

Author Michael Gerber coined the phrase, "Working *on* my business in lieu of working *in* my business." There is a significant difference between the two. Think about the guy who learns the plumbing trade and decides to start ABC Plumbing. Poof, he is in business; however, as a single proprietor, it is just him working *in* his business. Fast forward a few years, and ABC Plumbing has expanded to three vans and several tradesmen working for the company. Now, the proprietor needs to carve out time to work *on* the business; policy items, procedures, reporting, and so on. In the beginning, many times, it is just you.

That said, ten years is a long time to toil on something with no guarantees, but the fruits of my labor were well worth the wait. As I write this, we are now approaching our 15th year in business, and what a ride it has been! Anyone involved with a start-up business can relate. I am glad we hung in there, pushed through, and weathered the storms.

Apartments to Hot Sauce is a book about pushing back your fears and finding the courage to do what you want to do. That's exactly what I did with Urbane Apartments. I pushed back my fears, found my courage, and did what I wanted to do. If you have already tried something new but were unsuccessful and you are ready to roll your dice again, this book is about picking yourself back up and taking your second chance. I have been where you are now, and I get it.

Mostly, *Apartments to Hot Sauce* is simply my story; however, I hope you find a nugget or two that helps you to discover what it is that you truly want to do, find the courage to do it, and enjoy the journey along the way.

Chapter 2:
You Think You Have Time

If you have ever dated in your later adult years, the term "baggage" seems to surface frequently. The term could refer to kids, goofy family, failed marriages, failed work scenarios and so on. After completing a lot of personal development work during my life, the dirty little secret is that everyone has baggage, even people you wouldn't suspect. Maybe I should say that again; everyone has baggage! Some folks might camouflage it better than others, but it is still there. We all have baggage, even those one would never suspect. There is no normal. That is a complete myth.

It's fascinating how long we drag around our baggage. Our baggage becomes an anchor that we should focus on cutting loose. Is your baggage getting in the way of you starting your business? The looming question is, why haven't you started your BBQ shack, your book, your welding shop, or your cupcake bakery yet? What is your baggage? What are you afraid of?

I know a woman who loves talking about Kolbe testing, an assessment that helps people figure out their strengths based on various criteria. She enjoys her current job, but when she starts talking about Kolbe testing her eyes get bigger and you can see the energy radiating from her face. On a scale from one to five, if she were to gauge how she felt about her current job, it would probably be around a five, but ask her about Kolbe testing and BANG, it's off the charts! That's the only trigger you should really need to get involved in something you want to do.

When there's something that lights your fire, why aren't you striking the match? Is the reason because you are dragging an anchor? The danger is that, at some point, the anchor gets comfortable for us.

The preceding point is worth repeating and pondering. So, ask yourself; what lights your fire, and why aren't you striking the match?

In his book, *Turning Pro: Tap Your Inner Power and Create Your Life's Work*, Steven Pressfield says, "It's easier to be a professional in a shadow career than it is to turn toward your true calling." The payoff of living in the past or remaining stuck thinking about your future (but that's all you're doing) is you never have to do your work in the present. We are programmed to think that we need to remain plugged into our job, even if we do not like what we are doing, because of the security the job and the paycheck provide. The term "golden handcuffs" comes to mind. We hear that term a lot, but what does it really mean? Maybe it seemed like a great idea to upsize the house and purchase a new car at that time. We all seem to fall victim to that trap, but that is the very reason the man, our employers, can keep us chained down.

Business and employers have the upper hand and control over most of their employees through the money they pay them in the form of wages. The Man (insert your employer) tells you when you must come to work, how long you must work each day, and what time you can go home. The Man tells you how long you have to eat your lunch, and how many hours you can and cannot work this week. It is not a good or bad thing; it is just the way things seem to work when you have a job. To be clear, jobs aren't all bad. Some folks have little to no discipline, something the Man rarely falls short of.

Sidebar

"Often, the more money you make the more money you spend; that's why more money doesn't make you rich – assets make you rich." – Robert Kiyosaki

End Sidebar

It might look like you have everything you ever wanted, but do you really? Sometimes it's easier to just keep doing what you're doing than it is to follow your true calling, which is what you love to do and what energizes you. We buy into the belief that, before we can act, we must receive permission from someone else - a spouse, a parent, a boss, or a figure of authority.

Maybe needing approval is your anchor. It is for many folks. The problem with that is we typically don't ask the right people the right questions. Certainly, everyone has an opinion; however, we sometimes rely on feedback from someone who knows nothing about the topic and has no practical experience with the issue at hand. Asking a seasoned entrepreneur about the risks and pitfalls of a start-up will yield a much different consideration than asking Aunt Mary what she thinks. Often, we tend to seek advice, which may not really be advice at all, rather we're just seeking approval.

Many times, in my own life, the ideas that got the most 'no's' and the greatest pushback became the things I would double down on. There are naysayers everywhere. Be cautious of where and who you seek information from. If someone owns and operates six hardware stores successfully and gives you advice on starting your first hardware store, the odds are you should listen. If Uncle Roger, the unemployed factory worker, speaks, you may want to discount the information accordingly. You see, it gets a little tricky, because Uncle Roger only wants the best for you; at least that is what he says, and maybe even how it seems on the surface. So many times though, remember, everyone has baggage, and that baggage speaks, and directs us toward paths based on a plethora of agendas.

Sidebar

Double down: making a calculated gamble in order to maximize the potential yield of a project.

End Sidebar

So, does the pain of sitting in a cubicle outweigh your fear of tipping the scale toward your favor? Do you love what you do or are you resisting your calling? Resistance to your calling can actually derail your path for greatness. It might look like you have everything you ever wanted, but do you really?

There are countless Dads out there who missed too many little league games, kid's plays, special events, and so on, because they were tethered to the Man, to the job. That is not to say that the entrepreneur's path toward self-employment allows unlimited freedom, except it kind of does.

The power of choosing the time in which you come and go to work is much more profound than we are aware. Just try leaving your job at 2:00PM in the afternoon for a few days in a row and see how that works for you. You see, the "Man" is very clever. Human nature plays well into his strategy, as there are busybodies in nearly every workplace environment that happily play time clock police. To be clear here, this is not about working less, or screwing around more, it is merely about being acutely aware of the choices you have or do not have in your current environment. If it's okay to be like a herd of sheep, and that suits you, then all is well. If that doesn't suit, then perhaps starting to engineer something different is in order. It is remarkable how quickly the universe starts to answer our calling once we are aware.

Sidebar

You have to decide whether you want to make money or to make sense because the two are mutually exclusive." - Dr. R Buckminster (Bucky) Fuller

End Sidebar

Bucky Fuller is a fascinating guy and he talked frequently about procession, or the ripple effect of the things we do, and the effect of the things we do not do. The sidebar quote, *"You have to decide whether you want to make money or to make sense,"* was and has been life altering for me. Although this is a quote that is frequently used, it is often misunderstood. The quote represents a critical reason why Buckminster Fuller was so successful in making a huge difference in the lives of millions of people. It also explains how he earned an income of over $1,000,000 per year in the 1950's. The point here is this: we think we are working for money, but what if we shifted our focus and broke the chains of the anchor that's holding us back.

Look inside your heart and you will know whether or not you are hiding from your true calling. You will know if you are meant for better things and have turned away from your higher calling.

Does your face light up and your blood start pumping when you talk about going to work tomorrow? Or is fear holding you back? We all have fears, and there are no guarantees, but imagine a life where all your time is spent on the things you want to do. What if you could reclaim your time and give your greatest attention to a project you create yourself, instead of working at the directive of the Man.

I have few regrets in my life, but one of them is waiting to venture out on my own business later in life, as opposed to sooner. My anchor was shame and embarrassment, having failed at my first try in business. I followed my father's footsteps right off the cliff; however, that didn't mean I needed to continue to drag that anchor for close to 20 years before I cut it loose and tried rolling the dice again. I thought I had time. That is not to say that one shouldn't be cautious and take things slowly, but for me, decades went by because I thought I had time.

If you ask someone why they have not gone after their dream of leaving their current job or starting their own business, they will probably respond with a myriad of responses like, "I can't leave my job now. I'll do it when I have more money in the bank," or "I'll do it when the kids are older," or, "I'll do it when I'm older," or, "I'll do it when I have some more free time."

The trouble is, you think you have all the time in the world. So, you keep putting off what you want to do until hopefully that fateful day comes when you will suddenly have more time than you did before. The fact of the matter is that you have the same amount of time that everyone else has, including someone who is already actively going after their dream.

Time is ticking by whether you want it to or not. We all have the same 24 hours every day. At the end of the day, you don't regret what you did do, you regret what you didn't do.

One writer I know churned out many articles every day for a property management trade newspaper, but it wasn't what she wanted to be doing. She wanted to be a screenwriter. One day, her close friend asked her the most important question she's ever been asked. She queried, "When you're on your deathbed, are you going to wish you wrote one more property management article, or will you wish that you finished that screenplay you always wanted to write?" She knew the answer. From that point on, she found a little time every day to work on several of her movie ideas.

What in the world keeps you in your current situation? What you're doing must make you feel something. What is the payoff for staying? Maybe you feel important because you are earning a good chunk of change. Or maybe you feel accepted by your peers because of the fancy schmancy title you have. Maybe you're just trying to keep up with the Joneses, or have bills to pay, or kids in college, or not enough money in the bank.

The truth is, if you look into your heart, you know that you want to be an artist, but you chose to become an engineer. It paid more, and your parents (gotta love them) convinced you that it would be the smarter decision. Having a higher paying job helps you buy your home, pay for your kids' college, and fund your cushy retirement. However, every day you go to your job you ache, because you really would prefer to be painting at your studio.

Maybe you are waiting for someone, anyone, to tell you that it's okay to leave your job and start your own business (or at least start your business on the side). Your identity is seated in your own ego, and that ego is so weak that it cannot define itself based on its own self-evaluation. We allow our worth and identity to be defined by others. Maybe your mom said you wouldn't be able to support yourself as an artist, so you went with the safe route and became something that paid a lot more.

As I mentioned before, most of us crave validation. We are tyrannized by our imagined conception of what is expected from us. We are imprisoned by what we believe others think, how we ought to look, what we ought to do. We fear, above all else, becoming (and being seen and judged as) ourselves. In other words, just like I said at one point in my life, "If they really knew me, they wouldn't like me." Becoming your true self means being different from others; thus, possibly violating the expectations of the others, without whose acceptance and approval, we believe, we cannot survive. Paradoxically, we take ourselves and the consequences of our actions so seriously that it paralyzes us. Sometimes, we are numb for a decade before waking up again.

You might believe that before you can act, you need permission from someone, but again, the truth is that the only one who needs to give you permission to go after what you want is you. You do not need validation from your mother that being a writer, or an artist, is a viable business before you pick up a paintbrush or start writing that book. I had to spend most of my efforts pushing the naysayers out of the way. I got the label of being a bulldozer. "He just bulldozed the ideas through," people would say. Filter the people out of your life who do not have experience in that area or who will be a negative force when you are trying to accomplish your goals, no matter what those goals are.

We are trained early on to be grateful that we even have a job, and to work hard at it, and put money away, and it will reward us when it comes time to retire. Today, the truth is, that at any given time, someone in your company (The Man) can lay you off or fire you even after you have put all your blood, sweat, and tears into the job. So if not now, when? Next year? Five years from now? Twenty years from now? Imagine a life where you spend time painting, or baking, or designing the next best gadget that you will one day pitch on Shark Tank and earn millions from. Imagine working the hours you want to work and not the hours that your job dictates. When does that happen? It happens now. There is no other time than now. It is time to start building the business you always wanted – where you are the boss, doing things your own way. It is time to work for yourself and not some boss in a job you really do not want.

It is also time to perform a self-evaluation of your own happiness. Dr. Phil commonly asks, "How's that working for you?" Can you see the payoff? You are putting in a lot of time at that job, is it really what you want? What if you didn't have to go? What's your payoff for staying? Is your payoff a bigger home or more vacations? If that is what you want, then maybe you are in the right place. If you want your payoff to be something that you own or something that you can control, then maybe this job is not the place for you. You are making the choice to work for the other guy and not go after what you want.

If you ask most people why they're doing all this work, they'll tell you it's for money. By this, they mean a steady paycheck that provides security. Money is one of the primary reasons people take on thousands of dollars in college loans to get a degree for a high-paying job that they don't like and will spend most of their waking hours at — all while the things they really love in life sit on the sidelines waiting for them to finish working. The problem with this approach is that you only make money as long as you work. The only thing of value that you have to sell is your time. So, in order to make more money, you have to work longer hours, which is physically taxing.

Sidebar

An Asset: Property owned by a person or company, regarded as having value and available to meet debts, commitments, or legacies.

End Sidebar

Because you only have a finite amount of time and energy, as an employee, your earning potential is finite. Conversely, if you ask wealthy people what they work for, they'll tell you it's for assets. By this, they mean investments and businesses that provide steady cash flow each month with little-to-no work. Adding more assets is much different than working for a paycheck. For instance, adding assets doesn't require working longer or harder. In fact, the higher your financial IQ, the less you have to work to acquire high-quality assets. Assets then provide passive income, even while you're sleeping or playing.

I am not saying that you need to hand in your two weeks' notice right now; just decide that this is the right time to stop working for the other guy and start working for yourself. It is time for you to start your business, and it is time to take that first necessary step to get where you want to go. Things will start to happen, but only if you start shifting your thinking from 'want' to 'are.' It's no longer about what you 'want' to do – it becomes about what you 'are' doing. Ever wonder when a runner becomes a runner? It happens when he starts running. Ever wonder when a writer becomes a writer? It happens when she starts writing.

The point here is to shift your thinking, Cut the line to the anchor and lessen the drag:

- Let go of your baggage.
- Stop looking for validation.
- Stop looking for permission.

- Get started. Now!

You could achieve your own freedom by bypassing everything you thought was a prerequisite. You don't need to borrow money – you just start. You do not need to hire employees - you just start your project on your own.

EXERCISE #1

Finding Your Value Curve

Planning and strategizing are my favorite parts of starting a new business. One exercise that has helped us in the beginning stages of branding our business is called "creating a new value curve," which means looking at how your business strategy works in relation to your close competitors. Getting really clear with the answers to this exercise helped us to ferret out a niche in our boutique businesses.

Think about the circus business. For years, it was dominated by Barnum & Bailey Ringling Brothers. However, over the years, their business model greatly declined and a new start up, Cirque du Soleil, was launched. They turned the circus business on its head.

The traditional circus business model worked for over a hundred years, but selling tickets for five bucks to get in and see the animals was no longer working. Instead, the new model was to sell tickets to adults for $25 and compete with concerts and other quality adult events. They also dropped the biggest risk from the old model, the animals.

Recently, some new start-ups, coined as the "Sharing Economy," have also been extremely successful:

- Uber is now the world's largest taxi company, but they own no cars.
- Facebook is the world's largest media company, but they do not create any content.
- Alibaba is the world's largest retailer, but they carry no stock.
- Airbnb is the world's largest accommodation provider, but they do not own any property.

The point here is that all of these industries existed, but someone thought differently about them, and had the courage to push back the naysayers.

EXERCISE #2

Ask yourself these questions:

1. Which factors should be reduced well below the industry standard?
2. Which factors should be created that the industry has never offered?

3. Which factors should be raised well above the industry standard?
4. Which of the factors that the industry takes for granted should be eliminated?

Answering these questions really helped us carve out niche businesses with both our boutique apartment business and our hot sauce business.

Create Your Niche

Forever and a day, apartment operators across the land thought the only color that carpet came in was beige, the only color paint came in was off-white, and all kitchen appliances were white. However, with our Urbane brand we introduced color, texture, and style—and with that, our customers responded by paying us bigger rents. I can tell you that for the first few developments we did, the naysayers had a hay day poking at me. After the third or fourth development, not so much. After the fifth or sixth, we were leading the pack. You see, part of staying close to the status quo is that it's safe, but it is also boring, boring, boring.

Have You Asked Why?

This is a tricky one. We tend to race to *what* we do. That is much easier to identify. We gravitate to *how* we do it. The question of *why* we do it only gets answered by the remarkable brands. If we reverse the order and start with *why* we are doing what we are doing and keep that at the core center of our culture, we are heads above the rest.

People buy from companies because of *why* they do, not *what* they do. This is one of the explanations as to why great brands exponentially lead the pack. Many times, their competitors actually have a better product. Many times, the competition is better capitalized. Yet the company who best identifies what motivates them, and why they are doing what they are doing, runs circles around the pack. Take the time to identify your *why* way before you get to the *what* and the *how* and your result will be diametrically different.

The Right Time to Get Out of Perfectville

Remember what I said earlier about our emotions being jaded depending on our environment and how we were raised? We just do not pop out of the womb thinking that we need to be a perfectionist and all the stars need to align before we can do something we want to do. There never is a 'perfect' time to do something you want to do. NOW is the perfect time. Now is the only time.

About four years into building our company, my wife and I were actually living in 'Perfectville,' in an absolutely gorgeous Queen Anne Victorian home in a historic downtown neighborhood with a perfect

2.5 kids and a perfect life. Then, after sitting on that front porch with my kids and making the decision to roll the dice again, we both pulled the plug on corporate America. The next big decision was whether or not to stay in our Perfectville home or make our business work. We sold the house and rented an apartment.

I could have said that it wasn't the right time to leave my cushy job and start a business; either because of my grand salary, or because I had a large mortgage to pay, or because we finally had a perfect house for our kids and didn't want to leave, but no matter what, I knew it was the right time for me. Decades pass by while you are busy living your life and then you suddenly realize that something you really wanted hasn't happened yet. I didn't want that to happen to me again.

Although my wife was extremely supportive, things became tense at home. I was the man of the house, pun intended, but we no longer had a house. We were in our mid-40s moving into an apartment. I left a job where I was making great money with huge bonuses to build a startup business. I wanted a shot at creating wealth, but I was also embarrassed to be in an apartment after we had that beautiful Queen Anne Victorian house. There was a lot of shame in renting an apartment again. My "shame anchor" was showing its ugliness again, and it almost crushed me.

If we hadn't moved to an apartment for a few years (which allowed us to skinny through our personal debt), I would have crashed the boat. Dave Ramsey says, "Live like no one else, so you can live like no one else." I didn't expect to be renting when I was that age, but as a couple, you can either do these things separately or they can bring you together.

As we briefly talked about earlier, your fears may be what's stopping you. One of my fears was something I worried about in that Queen Anne Victorian – will we ever get it back? We were afraid that we would never have a house like that again if we moved ahead with our plans to downsize and start a business. Interestingly, years later we laughed at the fact that we wouldn't even want that crazy house back, but at the time that's how I felt. I knew it was time to go after my dream, no matter what.

I had my own fears, but I had to stop feeling afraid of renting. I couldn't think about what wasn't working. Instead, I had to double down on what was working—and that was trusting my instincts that it was the right time. You need to trust your instincts; that feeling you have to start your own business is the right time for it in your life too.

It was the perfect time for me to start this business, but admittedly it took time to get it off the ground and make enough money to live on. So, even though

I quit one job to start this venture, I ended up needing more money to allow me to continue building my business on the side. I started blogging and tweeting about business and, as a result, I met an entrepreneur from Atlanta who wanted to talk to me about what I was doing. I knew that I needed to do a deal with this guy who was in the publishing business for rental magazines. My wife told me that I was out of my mind and that this guy was not going to hire me.

Two and a half weeks later, I was in New York City making a deal for a part-time consulting gig!

Was it a failure that I had to resort to taking another part-time job while I was getting my business underway? The pessimist reader will think so, because they focus on what you do not have, but working part-time wasn't a failure to me, rather it was part of the path that I was on. Winston Churchill once said, "Success is not final, failure is not fatal; it is the courage to continue that counts." At that time, a defeat to me would have been closing up shop and going back to work for the man. Instead, that job filled what I needed at that very moment and allowed me to continue the pursuit of my dream. It also gave me significant exposure in the multifamily world, which would come in handy later.

So, is your glass half full or half empty? Are you success or failure conscious? What I learned from crashing my first business is that I didn't know how to manage money and I didn't have the courage to say, "Hey, I know we talked about this, but now things have changed." If I had just done that one thing, I might still be in that business. I had all the power, but I was stuck in my own fears and, believe it or not, I wanted my clients to like me. Even at a subconscious level, I allowed the customer to dictate to me. I was failure conscious. I learned from that.

Did you know that Milton Hershey started three candy companies before his famous company? Did you know that before George Steinbrenner had success with the New York Yankees, he owned the Cleveland Pipers, a basketball team that completely failed in the 1960s. After several more failures, Steinbrenner had the courage to continue and finally land success, with six World Series visits between 1996 and 2003, and a record as one of the most profitable teams in Major League Baseball. For me, the universe delivered all of my steps in perfect order, as long as I was open to them. I was willing to do whatever I had to do and learn the lessons I learned to get to where I am now. There have been lots of twists and turns in the road, but I was willing to navigate them. Now I'm looking in the rear-view mirror at everything I learned then, which is now with me today in a larger picture. It's time to show up on your path and start your journey. It's the right time.

Sidebar

Seth Godin coined the phrase, "You have to ship," but finally stepping off the dock can be tough, particularly if you are pulling the plug and quitting your day job to do it. Seth Godin is the author of 18 books about the post-industrial revolution, the way ideas spread, marketing, quitting, leadership, and most of all, changing everything. In addition to his writing and speaking, Seth founded both Yoyodyne and Squidoo.

End Sidebar

"Many of life's failures are people who had not realized how close they were to success when they gave up." ~ Thomas A. Edison

If you are a real entrepreneur, you are still reading. If you are a fauxtrepreneur, you're probably writing your resignation letter, considering which beach to surf, and how long to grow your beard. A fauxtrepreneur is a person who comes up with countless business ideas but never actually sees one out. God bless you, fauxtrepreneurs, because you are going to have a much nicer time than the real entrepreneurs who are up against it all.

There was a great article in Business Week some time back titled "What to do if Your Startup Is Failing." Jason Calacanis, the founder of Silicon Alley Reporter and Mahalo.com, offered advice from the trenches to entrepreneurs in trouble. I was really able to resonate with many, if not each one. They have been scenarios I have lived through on my entrepreneurial climb. Calacanis has faced the fall a couple of times and learned some things from the experience. He starts out, "The first time it happens, you're terrified, because everything you've done—all the effort and dreams—will probably be lost (like tears in the rain). The second time it happens, you're deeply concerned, but you know it ain't over until you're splattered on the boulders below. The third time it happens, you smile and say, 'let's get it on!'"

You see, there are two types of entrepreneurs in this world: real ones, and the folks who play entrepreneurs for some portion of their lives. From a distance, most folks can't tell who's who. In up times, when the market is flush with cheap money and unexplained exits, everyone looks brilliant. It's only when the tide goes out that you know who's naked, to paraphrase Warren Buffett.

The differences between the two types of entrepreneurs become clear when the fan and the manure meet. The faux entrepreneurs run for cover rather than dealing with the storm. They go back to their plush, somewhat mindless jobs as vice-presidents at companies working for the man, while the real entrepreneurs suit up and clean up the mess.

Having made my share of blunders starting out, and digging rather significant holes from my mistakes, I understand. Calacanis also wrote, "A year from now, the real entrepreneurs who have real ideas will be battle-scarred beasts who are capable of taking big, bold risks, and you will still be crying about what could have been, while attending back-to-back meetings about nothing at BigCo.com. Not that I am judgmental of fauxtrepreneurs, who create noise, distract investors from the real workhorses, are lousy at their jobs, and take no real risk in their lives. On the contrary, I love fauxtrepreneurs, because you create the foundation upon which real entrepreneurs grow."

At the start of my career, it wasn't easy to stand out, but by the time I had created two or three businesses and became a fixture in the multifamily industry, things got easier. Now, over a couple dozen years later, I've been in business, and I learned that longevity is credibility. I have started a few new businesses, and that is the easiest part. It is fun and exciting and there is a lot of energy, especially when business starts to pick up. Selling is fun.

Now that you are thinking about your exit from the rat race, it is time to put your idea to paper. Keep in mind that the idea stage of a start-up is much safer than the actual start-up. It is exciting to talk about your idea and you can vacillate for hours on end about this and that. It feels good, but actually launching your idea is a bit scarier because the stakes are higher. It is no longer just verbal masturbation. You have likely plunked down some dough to get started, either yours or someone else's, and now the pressure is on to make it happen. So, what are you waiting for? The time is now.

Chapter 3
Believe It and You Will See It

Get the vision right and the Universe delivers the rest.

Chrometophobia (also called Chrematophobia) is the intense fear of money. Whenever I start to talk with folks about an idea they have about a new business, a screenplay, a new restaurant or another new start up, they will typically preface the conversation with, "but I don't have any money." It is fascinating that people gravitate to what they don't have as opposed to doubling down on what they do have. We will talk more about that later. By the way, it is a myth that you need to have a lot of money to start a business, because you don't. My own experience has taught me that capital always finds the right deal and capital always finds the great idea.

Do you know someone who is always yapping about having the next big idea, yet never really follows through to make it happen? On the other hand, do you know someone who can execute one solid idea after another? Have you ever wondered why some ideas manifest and move to action while some fizzle out? As you think about your own idea that may work, you might think, "I'll believe it when I see it." That is contrary to much of what we have learned in this materialistic society. Materialism is not just the gathering of goods; it also includes the belief that if I can't sense it with one or more of my five senses, then it is suspect.

To manifest your idea, you need to see it first. The idea that you might choose to believe something before actually sensing it is considered daft. Nevertheless, such a so-called daft idea can lead to increased happiness and the possibility of manifesting the impossible. Impossible cures, improbable events, unexpected windfalls, and happy surprises await those who believe (or pretend or imagine) first. 'Fake it till you make it' and 'act as if' are just a few examples, but my favorite is 'thoughts become things'.

Separating the Sizzle from the Successes

Everything we do starts with an idea, and ideas come in a moment's time. Great game-changing ideas can happen while you are in the shower, or driving, or any other time you allow yourself to relax and let the ideas flow. We get excited about them, particularly when no one is looking, or we think no one is looking. As soon as we think someone is looking, something starts to shift and we begin to think about what may be missing from the idea and thinking about that becomes the death of great ideas. Instead, focus on what you have. It is a completely different mindset and way of approaching projects with a dramatically different result.

When you visualize an idea in your mind, there is never anything missing from the picture. You can shape that picture however you like. There is no committee needed for approval. It is just an idea, and there is little to no risk in an idea, particularly if we have yet to share the idea with anyone.

For me, as I would drive about town and see a cool building, my mind would drift to a place of what the property may look like once we developed it. I would start to get excited about it. Throughout the whole idea process, never once does what I don't have enter the equation; that would be silly. It is my idea. I can create and shape it into whatever I want.

Opportunities can be scary, so it might actually feel safer to think and rethink, 'what might be missing,' but when you start to focus on what might be missing, that is exactly what you find.

Ideas Start to Materialize

At some point, what you think about and the ideas that you have will start to present opportunity, and the rubber will meet the road.

Stand Out from the Competition

When you're thinking about your idea, how does it stand out against your competition and how can you improve the idea, so it stands out amongst your competition? Think about the pain points of your potential customer, which is a problem or need that a business or company aims to solve. We tend to bench ourselves against our competitors. The problem with that thinking is that it is a race to commodity sameness.

Imagine if Starbucks had breakfast sandwiches and McDonald's had gourmet coffee. Would these businesses stand out? With our hot sauce business, we started to give away free bottles of our hot sauce at festivals. My partners thought I was nuts. Everyone else gave away food samples with the product in it or as a dipping sauce. We gave away a whole bottle, and people loved it. The pundits suggested using the small 3oz bottles, not our standard 6oz bottle. Here is the deal, we heard back from more people, even to this day, who attested that is where they first experienced our hot sauce. You see, people don't throw some things away, and a full bottle of hot sauce is one of those things that gets kept. Even if they don't like hot sauce, they would give it away to someone else, a friend or neighbor, who does.

The biggest thing that happened is they talked about it, they talked about us, not once, but nearly every time they used the bottle until it was gone. They really felt as though they were given something. The payoff to our little hot sauce company for giving product away proved to be a significant traction point, and the cost was relatively low.

Step One: Change

As adults, we do not spend nearly as much time thinking about what we want. We think about what we don't want. For example, we do not want to go to work at that exhausting job that is physically and mentally draining us, and we don't want to be in debt anymore.

The problem is we are so busy in our adult lives that we do not have, or make, the time to go after what we do want. We wake up, work our 9-to-5 jobs, and then come home exhausted. Then we have to care for the kids and our household chores. Before you know it, the day is over and the chance you had to make a change is gone. You vow to try again the next day, but again, the day is over and the chance you had to make a change is gone.

When does the cycle stop? It stops when you change it. It stops when you fight the current and make the change to live your life differently. Some people call it their 'aha moment'. It's that moment in their life when they realize it's time to do something different before they wake up 10 years later with nothing to show for it.

There are flash moments in your life in which everything changes, and the stars start to align. Why didn't I decide to write this book five or ten years ago? It's almost like these long periods of time would go by and I just wasn't plugged in. Change happens in an instant, and in such a small spec of time, our direction changes. Live more by intention, and less by the direction of the wind. I have spent years, sometimes decades, asleep, oblivious of my intent. This only creates regret.

Once I decided to start Urbane apartments, I didn't know what was going to happen, but I could see the business. I knew that it was going to be a success. In that one moment, everything changed in my life. When you make the commitment to change, you will find that you can move mountains.

Get Out of Your Own Way

What stopped you from starting prior to now? Honestly, I have no idea what stops someone from going after their dream. It could be something that happened to you way back in your childhood. For example, maybe you fell off the swing when you were a little boy and now you're afraid to climb into a treehouse; however, you always wanted to be a treehouse builder, but that past episode is stopping you.

What are you telling yourself every day? Are you telling yourself you're a failure and that you can't do this? Words are powerful. Your story is going to be different from my story, but the bottom line is that you aren't getting what you want because you're not focused on it.

Like we talked about in chapter two, sometimes it's a lack of time that stops us. I was running two businesses when I finally thought about putting pen to paper. I really did not have time to put one more thing on my to-do list, but I wanted this book.

We really are good at coming up with all kinds of reasons why we shouldn't or couldn't do something. Maybe your mother told you that you would never amount to anything and maybe you believed her. Perhaps what you want to be is so risky that you're scared. How about spending time focusing on what you *can* do and *should* do. You need to get out of your own way and do it.

Step Two: See It

Visualization has been a significant part of this process for me. Much has been written on the topic, and some of it can seem a little like hocus pocus, but the truth (for me) is that anything of material value has come from first generating a very clear picture of the idea in my mind.

Jumping out on my own, the first commercial real estate deal I did was a small infill project in the town we lived in. I could see it in my mind, weeks and months before the parcel showed up for sale. I would spend several minutes each morning shaping the idea in my mind, applying emphasis on the details of the building and the colors, and seeing a finished, perfect product. Athletes and other successful people have used visualization for years.

Carli Lloyd of the U.S. women's soccer team credited visualization in her team's victory at the World Cup. Early on in his career, actor Jim Carrey used to visualize that he had movie offers coming in and that directors liked his work. He even wrote himself a $10 million check and visualized that he would cash it at some point in his career. It was exactly the amount he was paid for his role in the movie Dumb and Dumber.

Success comes to those who organize their thoughts with a clear sense of purpose, and then place intent behind that purpose. This is much different than goal setting because it involves creating a very, very clear picture of what you want. Build a mental picture with as many details as you can muster up.

Your directions will start to appear; people, places and resources will present themselves along the path you need to move your idea to fruition. Part of your success will be creating good habits. As I've said before, your habits define you. There are no silver bullets or quick money schemes (at least I haven't discovered any) but spending some time in silence every morning has paid really big dividends for me. I encourage you to try it.

For the past 15 years I talked about wanting to write this book, but it took years before I actually got started. I couldn't 'see' it happening. I had never written a book before. I was a businessman, and I had no idea what writing a book was all about. So, I couldn't see the final product that you are reading right now.

One day I went to my local bookstore and walked over to the business section. At that moment, among all of the other books on the shelf, I could see mine. It was a beautiful sight. My book, on the shelf with all the other great writers—and you, my readers, buying it and enjoying it. I knew it was time. When I finally envisioned my book on the bookshelf, I knew it was going to happen. I had a time (now) and a vision (the bookstore). Within one week, I had a publisher and a contract.

See it.

Believe it.

The Universe delivers.

What do you want within the next day? Week? Month? Year? Decade? Can you answer that? If not, how do you not know what you want? It's your life; you own it, and you should know what you want out of it today, tomorrow and 10 years from now. Do you have to see it before you believe it or do you start to believe it and then you see it?

In 1982, in Ann Arbor, Michigan, two college students talked about what it would be like to start a deli. Today, Zingerman's Deli pulls in $35 million a year. It took 10 years after their initial conversation for the co-founders, Ari Weinzweig of Chicago and Paul Saginaw of Detroit, to sit down and answer the most important question, "Where do you want to be in 10 or 20 years?"

In one interview, Weinzweig said, "I didn't have an answer to that question, but it started a year-long conversation that ended up with our vision written for what we could see 15 years into the future." Ninety percent of what was in that document actually came to be. In lieu of expanding and opening more delis in other cities, they opened Zingerman's Community of Businesses, a network of enterprises (all food based), each of which is run by on-site managing partners.

Zingerman's vision statement was brilliant, and creating your own vision statement will change your life like it changed theirs. What do you want tomorrow, next week, next month, next year, and 10 years from now to look like? Do you want a tailor business? It doesn't matter that you do not have the money for a brick-and-mortar store right now. Do you want to be a sportswriter? It doesn't matter that you are currently a nurse's aide and aren't even in the field. Write it down. What happens once you put it to paper is that the world starts to align with what you want.

Exercise - answer the following questions:

What do you want?
1. Tomorrow?
2. Next week?
3. Next month?
4. Next year?
5. 10 years from now?

Instead of a vision statement, you can also create a vision board, which is a collage of images cut out of magazines. These images are supposed to represent whatever dreams you have in life. Katy Perry once explained to MTV that when her teacher asked the class to make a vision board, she chose a photo of Selena, who had just won a Grammy Award. Fifteen years later, Perry was nominated for her first Grammy. "I knew where I wanted to be even as a young kid. I just didn't know that if I put one foot in front of the other, I would actually get there someday."

Spanx founder Sara Blakely talks about using visualization. She explained that her goals were, "To be self-employed, invent a product that I could sell to a lot of people, and to create a business that would be able to fund itself." Done.

There is a great deal of power in visualizing what you want; just ask any professional athlete, like Billie Jean King, or any Olympian who uses visualization.

Step Three: Feel It

Does your dream idea excite you? If it feels good, move forward. If it feels bad, redirect. Emotion is the fuel behind manifesting your path. When you have a clear picture of your dream, your universe starts to deliver exactly what you need to make it happen.

Emotion is the lever that tips the scale. If you don't feel it, the vision doesn't materialize. Remember, an emotion is always at work below the surface, and if that emotion is self-doubt and 'I am not good enough,' that is exactly what you will get. That is the fuel you are using to propel your intent.

Let's say that your vision statement says, "I want to own my own cupcake business." Now think about walking down the street and seeing a storefront with "Mary's Cupcakes" proudly displayed on the sign. You stand there proudly, admiring the sight. It's yours. Let that sink in. Did you smile? Does it feel good? Let that sink in DEEP. That is the magic. The more clarity you have with that thought, the faster your success comes. When you are really tuned in to the visualization of your success, you are clearly in ascension.

If you are writing out your vision statement or creating a vision board, it should spark something inside you. You will feel it. You will start to get excited. When you put emotion behind the image it starts to materialize. Some people call it 'the law of attraction,' but it truly works.

The Result Equals the Intent

Simply put, whatever you are thinking of is exactly what you are getting from the world. Let's say that you want to start your own travel agency, but you work for someone else right now and you have too much debt to leave a secure job and venture out as an entrepreneur. You tell everyone that you want to be a travel agent, but each week you do nothing to get yourself closer to opening an agency. Nothing happened. Why? You did nothing and you got nothing in return.

If, on the other hand, you signed up for a travel agency class and started studying maps of countries around the world, you are one step closer to becoming a travel agent. All you have to do is look in your metaphorical rear-view mirror. What have you done and what has the result been? If you are in a dead-end job and you got skipped over for a promotion, that is the result of your intent. Why? Did you do anything to change it? Did you look for a better job?

The most fascinating part about the results of your intent is that they can be changed by you. Deepak Chopra says that intention is the starting point of every dream. It is the creative power that fulfills all of our needs, whether for money, relationships, spiritual awakening, or love.

Every day you wake up, your day is filled with intentions. Do you intend on going through one more day unhappy in a career that you do not want, or is your intent to find a job that makes you happy? Do you intend to finally build that prototype of your new invention, or do you intend on letting another day slip away and the invention sit there as just a sketch in a notebook?

My behavior tomorrow is a direct reflection about what I'm thinking about today.

Behave

Behave the way you want to live. What was your behavior yesterday? That's what you were thinking about. My behavior tomorrow was a direct reflection of what I'm thinking about today. It's an exact, perfect reflection. Change your actions, change your thoughts; that's wrong. Change your thoughts first. It all comes down to three simple words:

BE

DO

HAVE

Success never starts until you have an outline in your mind of what you want to be, do, and have. If you're not sure you're on the right path, monitor what happened yesterday, last month, and last year. That's what you're being, doing, and having.

Don't like what you see? Change it. Write those things down. For example, you want to be a runner because being a runner will help you to lose weight or win the marathon you always wanted to run.

BE: Runner.
DO: Buy running shoes and start running.
HAVE: Weight loss and a marathon medal.

You have to be before you can do. You have to do before you can have.

Our Habits Define Us

In this chapter, I have asked you to change your way of thinking and speaking and do something that propels you toward what you visualize as your goal. That's not easy for everyone. Change takes time, and our habits define us. They are hard to break, but once you do, you'll be reaping better rewards.

Double Down

What are you good at? If you are going to achieve your dreams, it's best to double down on your strengths. What do I mean by that? Again, we tend to focus on our negative qualities and situations. You don't have enough money to start a business. That's a negative. You have a cousin who is willing to give you her bigger kitchen to make cupcakes so you can get your baking done faster. That's a positive strength. Forget about what you're not good at and what you don't have. Instead, double down on your strengths. It pays off in huge dividends. Everyone comes to the table with different strengths. If you're trying to be like everyone else, it's called sameness. It makes you the same. You get paid more when you are different.

Richard Branson started Virgin Airlines with a single plane. Doubling down on his strengths seems to have worked. He has been quoted as saying:

"When we started Virgin Atlantic in 1984, we had some great people and lots of good ideas about how to do things differently. Sadly, we did not have a lot of money to take it to the streets. Compared to the giant establishment players of the time—TWA, Pan-Am, and British Airways—we had a tiny fleet, if one plane qualifies as a fleet, and a miniscule advertising budget."

Exercise: What are your strengths?

1. _____
2. _____
3. _____
4. _____
5. _____

When you visualize your dreams in this chapter, remember that I am not asking you to think about how it's going to go, or what you don't have or how you can't get there; I am simply asking two questions:

1. What do you want?
2. How does it make you feel?

Chapter 4
The 'Yes' Movement

Like many people, I love Saturdays. I love the way they make me feel and I love how relaxed I am when Saturday rolls around. At one point, I thought about my personal life and made the decision that I want everything I do and every day I experience to feel like a Saturday. I only want to say yes to those things that make me feel like it's Saturday.

Shonda Rhimes is the creator of *Grey's Anatomy* and *Scandal*. She is also the executive producer of *How to Get Away with Murder*. She took a year away from the Hollywood lights to write *Year of Yes*, a book that chronicled her journey of saying yes to whatever came her way. This was after her sister challenged the self-professed introvert, who said no to so many things in her life, to say yes and see what happened.

In her book, Rhimes said that she learned several rules about saying yes, and one of them was to say, "yes to you." She tells the story of a man she loved but didn't necessarily want to marry. Her family kept pushing her and the more she thought about marriage, the more she ate. Rhimes was pushing her true feelings back, so her year of yes taught her to focus on saying yes to what she wanted, not what everyone else wanted for her.

A few years ago, Eric Schmidt, Google's executive chairman said this about saying 'yes' during his commencement address at the University of California at Berkeley:

"Find a way to say yes to things. Say yes to invitations to a new country. Say yes to meeting new friends. Say yes to learning a new language, picking up a new sport. Yes, is how you get your first job, and your next job. Yes, is how you find your spouse, and even your kids. Even if it's a bit edgy, a bit out of your comfort zone, saying yes means you will do something new, meet someone new and make a difference in your life, and likely in others' lives as well. ... Yes, is a tiny word that can do big things. Say it often."

When it comes to focusing, Steve Jobs once said, "The hardest thing... when you think about focusing, you think, well yes, focusing is about saying 'yes,' no," Jobs said. "Focusing is about saying 'no'. And you've got to say 'no.'"

That's true, you do have to say no sometimes, but I want to focus on saying 'yes.' Now, saying yes, in my book, doesn't mean saying yes often or to everything that comes your way; like Rhimes did or how Schmidt suggests. It just means saying yes to those ideas that give you good feelings and saying yes to that feeling that you get when you envision your business.

Remember earlier when you walked down the street and envisioned your storefront or walked into a store and envisioned your product sitting on the shelf? Remember how good that made you feel? That is pure magic, isn't it? It's time to say yes to the magic.

So, let's get back to the person we talked about earlier who wants to be a runner. That person finally got to the point where he woke up from his life and said, "Yes, I'm finally going to be a runner. Yes, I am going to buy running shoes." He went out and bought his first official pair of running shoes. Then he signed up for a marathon. "Yes, I am going to run in a marathon."

Unfortunately, if he really did it this way, it was, most likely, an utter failure. Why? Of course, he said yes to STARTING to do what he wanted to do, just as I advised, but now it's important to understand that to get from the start line to the finish line there are many steps you need to take in between. You don't just jump from one to the other.

Flex Your Muscles

First, once you have your idea, you need to assess your strengths and make sure that they align with what you want to do. If you are a runner, perhaps your strength is that you are very fast out of the box, but do not have the stamina for long races. Instead, to inspire you to start running, maybe you could sign up for a sprint race or a shorter race versus a full marathon. Use your strengths to get you where you need to be. You will still feel successful when you complete a shorter race. You are still training for the marathon, but you didn't fail right out of the gate. You want to run a marathon, but you can't run a full mile without getting winded. You're not ready yet. You're starting, and that's where you need to be. A whole marathon? Not ready. Go a little slower.

Have you always wanted to be a baker? Do you love the smell and taste of cupcakes? Have you always wanted to sell pies, but you don't know the difference between knead and flute? You're not ready. You can say yes to being a baker, but your next step is not opening a storefront or baking pies for a party. You should think about taking baking lessons, or enrolling in culinary school, or learning how to bake properly. Take another step closer to one day getting that business started.

Of course, there are 'overnight success stories' in business. Someone creates a product, it goes viral, and then boom, they are an instant success – both in business and financially. What you didn't see is the hard work that they put in before the business took off; the failures they had to overcome, the challenges they had to face, finding their way around, and the times that they had to stand back up again after falling down. Overnight success is a myth.

Angry Birds was finally a success after 52 attempts. Rovio, the company behind the game, nearly went bankrupt during the eight years it took before the game finally became a success. They could have said 'no' more, 'no' we give up or 'no' we can't do this anymore, but they kept saying yes. Did you know that WD-40 is named after the 40 experiments it took to get it right?

In most cases, it takes time to grow a business. You need one customer, then two, then 10 and so on. It takes time to build your brand. It takes time to get customers and it takes time to succeed.

Remember that it took me almost nine years to turn a financial corner in the Urbane Apartments business. Things went wrong along the way, and I had to fix them and learn from them. I failed in the beginning of my construction business because I tried to do things that I wasn't good at or that I didn't know how to do. It's great to say yes and it's great to start, but you need to make sure you're doing the rest right.

On the other hand, it's okay to go out and do something different and crash the car. Fifty percent of businesses fail in the first year, but maybe the reason it didn't work was because they didn't cut the anchor loose. It's okay to say 'yes' again just like I did.

To say yes, it's just as important to say no. I would rather focus on the things you have to say yes to versus the things you're saying no too.

For instance, my wife and I fell in love with Arizona, but the reason we are here is because I earned a contract to do consulting with a company. I have since been invited by the company to continue working with them on a long-term basis. I love working for them a lot, but I do not like the idea of going into an office every day. I don't like any piece of it. I dislike doing it so much that I can't think about doing it again. I had already gotten to a yes in my life. Yes, I wanted to not work in an office anymore; however, I needed to engineer my life to replace this income and this opportunity, so it fit well with what I wanted.

To replace the income, I thought about working in a retail store, but I knew that didn't fit with my attributes and experiences. I needed to increase my odds of success. You need to reduce your risk and exposure and increase your odds of success.

If you are now in a place where you're going to make the leap, it behooves you to take some time to think about what will increase your odds of success. If you were going to make cupcakes, do you have what it takes?

Chapter 5
The Power of Starting

Now you have an idea, you know how you stand out from your competition, and you can visualize where you want to be in the next [however] many years. You are now harnessed with the power of starting and the power of quitting. It could be either, or sometimes both, because for sure there are some things you need to quit doing, and some things you need to start doing. I tend to focus on the power of starting more than the power of quitting.

What does starting look like? It begins by creating something remarkable. Some of the key ingredients of remarkable, as defined by the legend Seth Godin are:

- Remarkable doesn't mean remarkable to you; it means remarkable to me. Am I going to make a remark about it?
- Being noticed is not the same as being remarkable. Running down the street naked will get you noticed, but it won't accomplish much. It's easy to pull off a stunt, but not useful.

Is the experience you are creating for your customer remarkable, and does your customer find value in the experience created?

When you really know what you want, set a plan to accomplish it. Let nothing stop you and you will be successful. When you really desire something so deeply that you are willing to stake your entire future on a single turn of the wheel, you are sure to win. One of the most common causes of failure is the habit of quitting when one is overtaken by temporary defeat. Do not be deterred by 'no'. Many of my greatest victories have come after several no's.

Business Behavior

With your vision statement in hand and your intention set, you now have a clear picture of what your business looks like. Now it's time to make it a brand—a logo, a tagline, and so on. To me, branding boils down to "how our business behaves." Use that as your starting point for your brand; how you want your business to behave.

As I gaze out my screened porch window on a lovely fall Saturday morning, I can't help but think about branding. Perhaps I am sometimes obsessed with the topic, particularly with our own businesses, about how important it is and how much it matters.

I am staring at our neighbor's new car. He is a GM engineer and always has the newest models. This one is a real beauty. It emulates and mimics a luxury sedan, on similar lines as a BMW or Mercedes. Sleek lines with a rich look. I like it, until ... I see it is a Buick.

I have nothing for or against Buick, except I would never own one. It was the brand my grandfather drove. It is old. Maybe that is just me and my frame of reference (except my wife said the same thing). The new Ford Taurus has some of the same issues. It's a really great looking car, but the Taurus brand screams 'average Joe family man'. Not that there's anything wrong with any of that, but when you are creating a brand for your business, stop and think about the image you are creating for your customers and prospects. Sometimes, those brand images last a lifetime.

You should be creating an image that aligns with who you are and what you want your business to be. Branding works, and it helps you stand out and away from the crowded grocery shelves, the crowded market your product or service is in, and the ever-so crowded internet. Good branding, sprinkled with a little public relations dust, gets people talking; otherwise known as word-of-mouth marketing (remember my job signs from earlier in my career?)

There is a name for every conceivable type of marketing around, and that can be a bit confusing for the small business entrepreneur. The marketing and branding gurus like it that way; confusion shelters their incompetence. There is a lot of bad advice being administered by the marketing gurus. Note that there is a difference between bad ideas and bad advice. At the Urbane Laboratory, our digital marketing and branding group has tried more than our fair share of bad marketing ideas. Some of them would even fall into the really bad idea folder. Testing things is one way to learn.

Marketing Magic

Start here: train, teach, and lead your organization to a fundamental understanding that it is always about the marketing, and that you are marketing your business in everything you do. With that, our chances of creating 'remarkable' increase exponentially. But that's what all the books tell you, right? Well, something interesting is emerging. Seth Godin coined the term 'tribes,' and small, medium, and large tribes are popping up everywhere. Our responsibility is to facilitate leadership of these tribes, and leadership, my friends, has nothing to do with control. You simply cannot control a message, but you can participate in the conversation.

For example, we started a company blog for our small business about three years ago. The result was that it only sputtered along at best. It wasn't until we, or I, got out of the way that it took off. We turned it over to a tribe—our most passionate customers. We recruited six staff bloggers, all of whom were either current or past residents. The rules were pretty simple—the Urbane blog is about cool and hip happenings, interesting establishments, and people in and around Royal Oak, Michigan. It is not about our company. Be respectful and be responsible for your posts and comments. That's it. Those were, and still are, the rules.

The results have been satisfying, and our traffic and following has taken off exponentially. We helped to shape the tribe, and leaders within our core group of evangelists have emerged to lead the tribe. Pretty cool!

Our blog, The Urbane Life, has caused lots of folks to connect with hip and cool local businesses. It's our give-back to the community. By providing the platform, we enable bloggers to post about hyper-local happenings and places. What is the payoff? Try this on for size... we are on the first page of Google, ranking number one for the search 'Apartments Royal Oak', which is one of the most used searches in our area. We now have over 14,000 visitors this month and we only have 360 units. I think the blog was a great payoff, don't you?

Branding on a Budget

Not all marketing is conventional. Small business owners don't always have the time or the budget to use generally accepted marketing practices. Instead, they find that guerrilla marketing is more effective. "Guerrilla Marketing" as coined by Jay Conrad Levinson in his popular book, *Guerrilla Marketing*, is an unconventional system of promotions on a very low budget. The concept relies on time, energy, and imagination instead of big marketing budgets. Call it "street marketing," if you will.

I own and operate a small business after having worked in corporate America. I can attest to the effectiveness and efficiency of "Guerrilla Marketing". We are regular practitioners, and I'm here to share with you an example of tactics we have embraced, as well as another highly successful example on a more commercial level. Guerrilla marketing can be a very effective tool for your new business too, as it helps even the playing field. When executed well, guerrilla marketing propels your brand awareness forward.

We own and operate a small boutique apartment management business. A typical way that multifamily operators market units for rent is either print ads in newspapers or print ads in small booklets that are distributed at grocery stores, video stores, and the like. While these venues work fine for some companies, they are very expensive, which creates a barrier to entry for smaller companies that simply do not have the budget for such marketing avenues.

Our target demographic is young professionals, sometimes referred to as Gen X and Gen Y. They are somewhat nocturnal; in that they are out at night as much as by day. From my corporate travels, I had viewed a building in Minneapolis that had blue LED lighting around the top perimeter of the building. You can see it from miles away, and LED bulbs are very efficient. That building with the blue lights stuck in my mind. As we started acquiring apartment buildings on infill urban sites, we added blue LED lighting to every property. We even made the LED lighting a part of our brand. Cost: minimal. Effect: significant. Every one of our buildings became a visual billboard at night. I consider this our "Guerrilla Product Packaging" with the added effect of increasing brand awareness.

Upon launching a little larger project, we tried another very inexpensive LED lighting trick, with big results. We had a local artist create silhouettes on vellum paper that could be moved around and posted in the windows as units rented. We put a lamp with a blue bulb behind each silhouette to create a blue glow at night. The effect was overwhelming, stopping traffic and nearly every passerby. For a cost less than $650 for this idea, we successfully rented up 39 apartment units by creating a lot of "buzz."

You too can implement tactics like this with a little creative thinking. These ideas, and others, have allowed us to create a local brand on a shoestring budget. It isn't just about the low cost. As Levinson preaches, guerrilla marketing is about relying on time, energy, and imagination—instead of big marketing budgets.

Guerrilla marketing takes on many forms and functions, such as Blendtec's very successful, "Will it blend?" videos. *Will it blend?* became a viral marketing campaign of infomercials demonstrating the Blendtec line of blenders. In the show, Tom Dickson, the Blendtec founder, attempts to blend various items in order to show off the power of his blender. Dickson started this marketing campaign after doing a blending attempt with a box of matches. The phrase "Will it blend?" has become an internet meme.

While Dickson originally started with an infomercial, and certainly not all campaigns take off the way his did, good and creative ideas can become viral on a local level. Your ideas can too. Using YouTube as a conduit is one way to begin to showcase your product value and connect your product offering to your intended customer base.

Exercise

You frequently hear that deals are done at the table on the back of a napkin, and that would be true of my experience too. What that means is that you meet a potential contact while sitting in a restaurant or at a bar, and that person wants to know about your business. Suddenly, you have to explain to that person what your business is about, so you write the brief version on the back of a napkin. You need to be able to tell that person, in 30 seconds or less, exactly what your goals are and exactly what your business plan is. Get your pitch down, so that when opportunity knocks at the door, you are ready.

Pitch: Finish these sentences:

My business is_____.

My goal with the business is to _____
_____.

My customers would be _____
_____.

Over the next year, I plan on _____
_____.

Now, put it all together. For example, my business is Sal's Catering, and my goal is to bring an authentic Italian catering business to the neighborhood. My customers are those who want to have private events and corporate functions as well as special events. Over the next year, I plan on growing my business to include 10 new regular clients and I plan on hiring 2 new employees.

That's your pitch.

End Exercise

Customer 101

Soon, you will actually be working directly with customers. You need to take time to evaluate what will engage and delight your customer based on this brand you have now created.

At our local Mini Cooper dealership, they invite customers to bring in their beloved pets to the dealership, which some folks get really excited about. It works for the Mini Cooper brand, but you would not likely find that going on at the Jaguar showroom. Mini Cooper is matching a customer experience to the brand. This example has no correlation to Luxury and doesn't get better by adding more money.

Southwest Airlines, you either love them or hate them with their cattle-call lines, no assigned seats, and no frills. Yet true Southwest customers like, enjoy, laugh with, and have a favorable experience with Southwest. Herb Kelleher, the co-founder, chairman emeritus, and former CEO of Southwest Airlines, somehow figured out how to deliver a consistent, value-driven experience and he permitted his employees to fix it when it wasn't. Southwest employees behave differently than Delta employees. That is branding. That is how a business behaves.

In our boutique apartment management company, Urbane Apartments, we have used some innovative ideas to create our own remarkable experiences for our residents that align to our brand.

Here are some case studies:

- Thumbs up: The lease, a floor plan, emergency numbers, and some unit pictures are given to the resident on a thumb drive at move-in, which is also a keychain with our logo on it. Being able to walk away with all of the lease information on a tiny thumb drive that fits in their pocket and that they can also use to store additional information has created a "cool factor," or something worth talking about. This same idea may not bode well if we were in the senior housing business, but it does resonate well with our target demographic at Urbane Apartments.

- Urbane loves pets: We have embraced "Urbane loves pets," which has no extra fees, no breed restrictions, and no size requirements. Our theory is that if we have great residents, they likely have great pets. While there are certainly problems that occur from time to time, we own the local pet market segment by creating a favorable experience for our pet loving residents.

- Freedom Lease: Urbane created the "Freedom Lease," which affords maximum flexibility on lease terms for our residents. Today, lots of folks out there are consultants, and the standard one-year lease did not fit this paradigm shift. We have fostered a living arrangement that works to address our residents' needs and our needs. This living arrangement allows flexibility, which evokes a better experience than figuring out how to break a lease when circumstances change.

- Everyone loves treats: Anyone who has pets knows they love treats. Gus is no different, he lives for treats. Based on this concept, we knew that our residents would love treats too. So, we have developed a pretty interesting program—Urbane VIP cards. They resemble a credit card and enable the holder to cash in on several local discounts. During the tour, we go through the program, explain the benefits, and send them off with an Urbane VIP card. I am pretty sure our competitors aren't forking over any treats. It is a great way to differentiate, and it is funded by the local commerce.

- Make it playful: Apartment hunting is not a walk in the park. We have a centralized leasing center, known as Urbane Underground. It is anything but typical. There are farm watering troughs with tropical plants in them, a 45-foot-long bamboo planter, crazy music is playing, and a tropical bird is hanging out. There is a conference table that hangs from the ceiling with no legs. It's anything but typical. The point is, it is very whimsical and fun. Lighten up your approach, have some fun along the way with your business. Life is short.

- Make me laugh: Our marketing and branding at Urbane is anything but typical or traditional. We set up movies that reverse play against a backdrop that show silhouettes of girls dancing together, guys dancing together, and a variety of other wacky stuff. We can set up the movie in minutes, and it comes on at dark and shuts off at 2 a.m. Cars and people literally stop in the street and stare. They laugh, and make lots of comments about Urbane, including some who think that two guys dancing together is too provocative. We like that. Create marketing material that causes your prospects to talk about you. Is your marketing material causing your prospects to talk about you, or does it end up in the trash because it is outdated, old, and stale? By the way, the movie cost us nothing to make and we reuse the projector over and over.

Sidebar

The Four P's of Marketing: The marketing mix is often crucial when determining a product or brand's offer, and is often associated with the four P's: price, product, promotion, and place.

End Sidebar

Engagement and Emotion

We have now all heard about the four P's of marketing, but what about the two E's: Emotion and Engagement. Are you fully utilizing them? As we mentioned above, when we decided to go after the pet market and accept pets at Urbane, we stood out among our competition and added emotion to our customers' experience. Lots of places accept pets, but with weight and breed restrictions and a hefty pet deposit. Instead, we decided to keep it simple. We love pets at Urbane. There are no fees and no breed restrictions. The theory was this – if we have a good resident, they likely have a good pet. If we have a bad resident, they likely have a bad pet. We worked really hard on an enhanced resident screening system and on attracting great residents, which has also improved our collections. It's a nice side benefit to accepting pets!

The success of this program isn't about accepting pets, it is about "Urbane Loves Pets," which has successfully evoked prospects and residents' emotions. Consequently, we own the local pet market. If you are going after sliver markets, go with a vengeance and own them.

Start Anyway

Was Jeff Bezos stupid when he started Amazon.com? Some folks sure thought so, but he started it anyway. While I am not comparing our apartment business to Amazon, we were told by many that we would never, ever achieve the rents required to substantiate the product and brand that we were building. At about the fifth or sixth new Urbane community we developed, they stopped saying that. Remember to double down on your strengths and forget the rest.

"Sensible" is not the best metric for your ideas but start them anyway.

The natural tendency is to recoil from these ideas, because everything inherent to that kind of creativity requires breaking away from the norm, going against the grain, and leaning into risk and fear.

Wet the clay sculpture. Smear black seeds all over it. Watch them grow into green fur all over the sculpture. What a stupid idea, but they started it anyway. Now, half a million Chia Pets are sold each year.

- Western Union didn't want to buy Bell's invention, the telephone, because it had no value.
- Financial experts called Henry Ford's invention a fad.
- Fired from the newspaper where he worked because he lacked imagination, Walt Disney turned to other things.
- Elvis Presley was asked to leave the Grand Ole Opry after a single performance because he was "goin' nowhere."

The so-called experts said nobody would want to listen to digital music files. They said they couldn't be sold. Watching homemade television shows or having video chats with people on the other side of the world were all considered impossibly stupid ideas, even after they were proven feasible.

It's a well-kept secret in modern business that the purpose of analysis is to find a way to say "no" to things. In their seminal work, *In Search of Excellence,* Tom Peters and Bob Waterson pointed out that businesses that left slack for experiments, even dumb ideas that might not pan out, were the ones who struck gold with strokes of genius.

As Richard Branson says, protect the downside. Your stupid ideas might be the best ideas you've ever had. It's easy to assume that the brilliant ideas, which have shaped the world we live in, were recognized by both the creators and their peers and hailed as genius from day one. I don't know of a single case where that's true.

Before things are considered normal, they're new. And before they're new, they're just stupid, but start anyway.

"If your stupid project becomes successful, it will likely become accepted, then considered smart, and then standardized, and eventually, normal. Do not worry about people stealing an idea. If it's original, you will have to ram it down their throats."

When you can't let go of an idea, when you lose sleep over it, when you simply cannot not do it, that stupid idea has every chance of becoming tomorrow's normal. Your willingness to pay the price in blood, sweat, and tears will prove to yourself and to others that maybe it's not so stupid after all. It's the power of starting.

Chapter 6
Goaltending

They say, to be a success in life, you need to set goals. A lot has been about goals and goal mastery. My experience is that there is no silver bullet, and goals can be a double-edged sword.

Sidebar

From the notion that if two sides of the same blade are sharp, it cuts both ways. When something can have both favorable and unfavorable consequences, the term double-edged sword is often used to describe it. "Corporate lay-offs are a double-edged sword. The company saves money by not having as many salaried people on board, but has to pay more overtime ...

End Sidebar

In basketball, goaltending, as defined in Wikipedia, is the violation of interfering with the ball while it's on its way to the basket and it is (a) in a downward flight and might not go in, (b) entirely above the rim and has the possibility of entering the basket, and (c) not touching the rim. Type-A personalities, which so many entrepreneurs have, make them goal setters, yet some never reach the target; instead, they goaltend in lieu of tending to their goals. They goaltend by having an exhausting to-do list, disguised as a goals list. They are still dragging their "baggage", and they haven't cut loose the anchor yet. Often, we hold on to things, even when they no longer serve us.

"Becoming 'awake' involves seeing our confusion more clearly." ~ Rumi

I think the larger issue is to keep shaping the images in your mind, much like a sculptor shapes a block of clay into something spectacular. Before the artist paints, he sketches a rough outline, and before the rough outline, there is a mental image. Once you have clarity of the mental image, you will better recognize the clues along the path to success.

I am a proponent of writing my goals down on paper. Putting pen to paper elevates the score and plants a stake in the ground, marking your starting point. Different things work for different people. Some time management gurus preach to have every last detail documented. My preference is to create a chronological list from the mental picture and the vision statement.

Goals can be a double-edged sword if they become too rigid. Keep your list flexible. For me, most of my better opportunities along the path have come not from how good my goals were, but how clear my image of what I wanted was. My ability to match people, places, and things that cross my path and fit them with the mental image and vision statement has helped tremendously as well.

What about those intangible goals, like happiness; how does that translate to your goal list? In my case, one of my goals was to have every day feel like a Saturday. How do you define goals for something more abstract and intangible? Well, you need to engineer your life structure to meet that criterion. A part of true goal setting involves removing things from your day. We tend to think about goals as a list of tasks we need to get done in order to get the prize, when, in fact, many times the most value is in stopping doing something.

The Value in Taking Away

One of my goals is to increase the yield of office staff at our apartment communities and break the mold on the notion of one office staff person per every one hundred units.

For years and years, a myth has prevailed that one person for every one hundred units should be required. So, a three-hundred-unit apartment community would have three people on staff in the office.

I participated as a judge for the Arizona Multi-Housing Association for the property manager of the year award recently. We interviewed nearly 40 applicants, some of which were very bright, but something odd struck me after so many interviews in a condensed time frame. Why was there so much site staff? A couple of the questions we asked the candidates addressed the topic of change, and how it affects the sites and whatever the next big thing in the industry would be.

Most of the applicants' answers referenced technology, but NONE of the applicants referred to that technology as lowering expenses. In fact, the typical nonsense of (1) on-site office staff per (100) units seems to be growing, as each applicant had to also state their unit count and the size of their office staff.

My point here is, IF we have more technology, which we do thanks to the internet, property management software systems and so on, why have we not reduced the staff size at the properties? Otherwise, all this technology isn't really changing anything. We simply must stop asking our staff to do more, without first taking something off of their plate.

Key takeaway: Balance your goals list with addition and subtraction. Sort through the confusion and realize that all goals are adding things to your to-do list. Adding, by itself, only leads to chaos.

Signposts Along the Path

The Universe will put signposts in your life. You can either ignore them or embrace them. You can choose and wish for all the things you want, but the things that are coming to you, you will never be able to hide from, and the things that you want so badly that are not supposed to be for you for whatever reason, they'll never come to you.

Being awake and aware of your surroundings is prudent if you are in an unfamiliar place, but it's also useful on your entrepreneurial journey. If the purpose of your goals is to create a path and keep you focused and organized, make sure you are flexible enough to see, and moreover, act on the signposts. More on that later, as it is ever so important in nearly every successful entrepreneur's journey.

If your goal is to become a public speaker, it would be helpful to be aware of opportunities that cross your path relative to that, such as an article listing the top ten ways to pitch to be a guest blogger, or how to pitch the top ten business magazines for a guest article. The content within those articles would be useful knowledge in helping prepare you to position yourself as an expert in a certain field. This might ultimately lead to a speaking engagement. So, one of your goals could be to send out two guest articles a month to prominent bloggers in your field of expertise with a request to guest blog for them. Guest blogging, in this case, would help propel your exposure to a new audience. Perhaps your writing may be read by someone outside of your existing sphere of influence.

There is a lot more to goal setting than just picking a goal and moving forward. While that is important, it's also important to ensure that you are setting the right goals at the right time so that you can truly be successful and watch things unfold in alignment with your vision statement.

In order to ensure that you are setting the right goals for yourself, think about this question:

Is it realistic?

With a little research you can ensure that your goal is realistic. If you're not sure if something is actually achievable, then perhaps you've not done enough research. Once you've set a goal that is indeed realistic, then you need to be specific enough in your description of it so that it's also easy to reverse engineer the goal, working backwards to create a schedule of actions needed to succeed.

Multifaceted Approach

Your life is multifaceted, so your goals should be broad-spectrum and cover many areas of your life in order for you to feel successful. If you have a wonderful business and career but your personal life suffers, then no matter how successful you are, you will not feel successful. Something will always feel as if it's missing from your life if your goals aren't inclusive. Therefore, make sure your goals include something from each aspect of your life.

Real Need

Once you create the schedule, including a timeline and dates to reach each goal and milestone, you need to truly consider how representative it is of reality and how closely it aligns with your vision statement. Say your goal is to write a business plan in six months, but you haven't set aside the time needed to research. If you don't schedule in the time needed, you won't succeed because something will always be in your way or consuming your time. It will be very frustrating to practice your schedule because it doesn't represent reality.

Adjust with Setbacks

Many times, when setting goals and schedules, instead of learning from failure, we give up. Once you implement your schedule to reach the goals that you have set, and when you notice there are things you've forgotten to take into account, don't give up, adjust. Learn from the failure and change the schedule to be more realistic.

You might find that, in practice, you have to rewrite all your goals and your schedule, but this is perfectly acceptable. Many people believe failure is something negative, but the truth is, if you don't fail sometimes, you're not going to learn much, and it's likely your goals are too easy.

Your Goals or Someone Else's

A lot of people set goals that represent what someone else wants instead of what they want. This scenario can really cause a lot of bad feelings and resentment, which can derail the best laid plans. As you set *your* goals for *your* life, ask yourself if they're really what you want for yourself or what someone else wants for you. Ask yourself, are you okay with any goal you make being for someone else before you embark on your own journey?

It's okay to do things because of someone else, but it's important that you are honest about that. Just make sure to make some goals for yourself too that don't involve anyone else's needs or wants.

Stay on Track

Schedules and timelines are very important to the success of reaching any goal in life. Work and tasks fill the allowable timeline. Inspect what you expect. This mentality works well with your own self-examination, as it does in managing projects. To-do lists pale in comparison to a well laid out calendar of tasks and activities that get you from point A to point B. Ensure that you look at your schedule every morning and every night and note when you succeed in sticking to your schedule and when you don't. Noticing a pattern of activity can be helpful in fixing a poorly written schedule. Also, make sure you're staying realistic about whether or not you're sticking to the plan.

Sidebar

My Dad used to say, "Work fills the allowable time space." Goals and their timelines are no different. While it need not be a race, do not drag things out with over-extended time frames.

End Sidebar

You Get What You Think About

If thoughts turn into things, then when writing a goal, it's important to write it in a positive way, or at least in a way that feels positive to you. When writing down a goal, change the words to sound more positive and see if it is more motivating.

Just as setting too few goals can be a problem, so can setting too many. Everyone has a personal life, a career life, and points in between. If you have set goals in too many areas of your life at once, you might tire yourself out and get overwhelmed. Instead, pick one personal goal and one other type of goal to focus on until you achieve them. Then you can add more goals as time goes on. You don't need to do everything today. A great motto to remember is, "slow and steady wins the race."

Sidebar

"Get the big rocks right first and you can make time for the important stuff. The secret is to prioritize," says Stephen R. Covey in his book, "First Things First".

Imagine you have a jar. You want to fill this jar with some rocks and some sand. What's the best way to do it?

One way is to add the sand to the jar first and then add the rocks. If you did this, however, you'd quickly find that it's impossible to make everything fit. With a layer of sand at the bottom of the jar, there's no room for the rocks.

On the other hand, if you begin by putting the rocks in the jar, when you pour in the sand it will sift downward to fill in the gaps and the cracks between the rocks. Everything fits.

End Sidebar

Setting the right goals for your dream takes some thought and consideration. Don't try to set all your goals in one day; instead, set some goals in different stages and in different areas of your life. Give a lot of thought to why you're making the goal in the first place.

Many use the acronym S.M.A.R.T. for goals. It can help you make better goals. Each letter stands for a different area of the goal. If you create a smart goal, you have created a goal that is Specific, Measurable, Actionable, Reasonable, and Timely. Using SMART goals can set you up for success in your goal setting.

S stands for specific. This means that your goal needs to be spelled out very precisely. Using language that leaves no doubt as to what the goal is, why you want to achieve the goal, and how you will get there is very important. If you are not able to detail the description of the goal, it will be hard to meet it. Take the time to do this part right.

M stands for measurable. There should be a metric that you can use to determine success. If your goal can't be quantified, then it's not a full goal and you won't know how to tell when you've succeeded.

A is for actionable, assignable, or achievable. The preference to really get something good done is to make your goal actionable, meaning something that you can take action on each day that will eventually result in an accomplished goal. Goals should also be achievable, or you will only get frustrated. Be accurate about the time it takes to reach a goal, and what actions it takes to get there. Also, know who will be responsible for doing it.

R can stand for realistic or relevant. If you want your goal to be achieved, it should most certainly be something that is realistic, or you will fail. It should also be relevant to your vision statement and match your values.

T is time-bound, timely, and trackable. All of these are important parts of the goal creating and setting process. If you don't set a time limit, and you can't track what is happening, your goal will be hard to quantify or achieve. The important thing is that you need to have a process to help you make smart goals. Smart goals are goals that you follow through on, achieving and recognizing when you've met them.

Everyone has conscious and subconscious ideas that can become limiting beliefs. These ideas stop us from achieving our goals, if we let them. Sometimes these beliefs are instilled in us during childhood and sometimes we create them ourselves.

An example of a limiting belief that can get in the way of your success is how you see yourself with money. If you believe you will always struggle and will always be poor, chances are you'll set yourself up for failure. Your limiting belief that you're poor and that you will always be poor becomes a self-fulfilling prophecy.

The same can be said about anything negative in your life that limits you; whether it's career, education, or personal life, such as being healthy and of normal weight. If you see yourself a certain way, it can be hard to change that view and let go of that limiting belief.

There are eight telling phrases that point to a limiting belief:

1. Hopeless: Any time you use the word 'never' is a clue that you're focusing on a limiting belief. For example: I will never have any money because you need money to make money. News flash... You DO NOT need money to make money. You need great ideas to make money.
2. Helpless: When most people feel uneducated or helpless, they blame their circumstances

instead of working to change them. I can't manage my money because I don't know how. This excuse sounds insightful, but the part that is missing is the feeling of helplessness. All you need to do is take a personal finance course.

Sidebar

An example of moving from financial helplessness to "knowing", as Robert Kiyosaki tells us, a key to becoming financially literate is to understand the difference between an asset and a liability.

Many people think they know what an asset is. Accountants use one definition that requires lots of financial calisthenics. Another definition that's grounded in simplicity and reality is: An asset is anything that puts money in your pocket and a liability is anything that takes money out of your pocket.

End Sidebar

3. Useless: The idea that nothing you do will make a difference and you believe that any action you take won't make a difference. It doesn't matter if I work out an hour a day, I won't lose weight anyway. How do you know? Have you tried to do anything for longer than a couple weeks?

4. It's the Universe: Sometimes a limiting belief has to do with the idea that forces outside of your control are at work to keep you down. You can't find a job or get clients because the economy sucks, where you live is depressed, you don't have the right clothing and so forth, but you do nothing in your power to change it because it's your destiny. The "everything happens for a reason" type of thinking can be very limiting and make you feel powerless.

5. Worthless: The idea that you're not smart enough or good enough to do what you really want can be a very strong limiting belief. This seems to affect women more than men. You feel you're not pretty enough, smart enough, or good enough to have something, so you don't take the steps to achieve it, because you don't feel that you deserve it.

6. Genetics: While there are certainly some instances where genetics play a huge role in a person's life, the truth is that almost everything that is genetic can be fixed with the right mindset, training, exercise, and outlook. You're not stuck with your genetics, but if you think you are, you may not try anything to pull yourself out of the rut you're stuck in.

7. Failure: The truth is the fear of failure is a common limiting belief that many people share. "I'm a bad public speaker, so if I do it,

I'll be judged. I'll fail anyway, so why try?" These are common refrains. How can you set a belief in stone if you've not tried?

8. I am different: The most limiting belief about being different is that different is bad. You don't want to be who you are because you're different and you'll be looked at as different by other people. You're afraid to be who you are, and because of that you don't even know who you are, and you're too scared to find out due to the fear of rejection or ending up alone.

If you ever hear any of these phrases go through your head, try to disconnect from them, and turn them around to "why not me, instead of why me." Always ask yourself, "why not me?" The truth is, you're not feeling anything different from anyone else who has made goals and achieved them. The difference is in the doing, not the intelligence or talent.

Many people have issues with goal setting due to placing limiting obstacles in their own way. Some of the most common barriers to goal setting involve fear and lack of belief in yourself. This is crippling enough to thwart your efforts to even set a goal, much less follow the steps toward achieving it. Perhaps if you know some of the most common goal setting obstacles, you can work toward overcoming them.

You Don't Want What You Think You Want

Some goals are set because other people want them for you. If you don't really want what you say you want, it will be very difficult to set a goal for that particular thing. Be sure you've set the goal for the right reasons and that it is something you really want. Write down the pros and cons of any goal and know why you want to achieve that result before setting it in stone.

You Don't Truly Understand the Importance of Goal Setting

Many people think goal setting is just hocus pocus and doesn't really work. If you don't really understand the power behind appropriate goal setting, it can be hard to take the time out of your day to truly set a goal. To understand the importance of goal setting, read several books about success and you'll find that the most successful people set realistic goals, and then work that goal into their schedule every single day.

Even people who experience overnight success didn't really achieve everything overnight. It was many nights of following a plan that brought results.

You're Not Really Sure How to Set a Reasonable Goal

If you've actually tried to set a goal before but didn't experience results, it's probably because you just don't know how to set a goal. It's not as easy as just writing down a dream. Goals aren't dreams; they are realistic, specific, achievable end results that you want to see. Take the time to learn the best goal setting techniques in order to experience goal setting success.

You're Scared of Failure

Many people do not bother setting goals because they have a self-limiting belief that they'll fail anyway. Therefore, if they do not set a goal, they won't have to endure being a failure. Remember that the idea of planning to succeed over planning to fail is realistic. No goal setting is a recipe for failure; goal setting is a recipe for success. When you accept that you can only achieve real success through goal setting, you'll overcome this obstacle.

You're Afraid of Judgment

Sometimes people are scared to set a goal for something because they see it as outrageous. For instance, let's say that you want to go back to college to get a master's degree, or you want to start your own business. You fear that if you set that goal, and other people know about the goal, they'll judge you harshly for wanting it or for some other imagined issue. If you are worried about what others think of you, it's time to dig deep inside yourself and get over it. The truth is, what you think of yourself is more important than anything else. When you stop judging yourself, you'll stop worrying about the judgment of others.

You're Afraid of Success

Believe it or not, some people are literally afraid of success. They feel too much pressure surrounding success to actually make the goals that will make them successful. They are more comfortable in their role as someone who is not successful, or who is 'normal', instead of as someone who sets a goal, works toward achieving it, and is seen as a success. The truth is, there will always be people who want to tear you down once you achieve some success. The saddest thing in life is regretting not doing something. Most people regret the things they did not do more than the things they did do - right or wrong.

You Secretly Don't Think You're Worth It

This is where the way you see yourself is really important. If you see yourself as someone who doesn't follow through, who doesn't succeed, and who can't change their life, you'll avoid goal setting like the plague. You're the only person on Earth who can control your actions. So, you're the only one who can set the goals for you, and the only one who can make yourself feel worthwhile.

You Don't Really Believe It's Possible

People avoid goal setting because they simply do not see the vision of what can be. They don't believe. They don't fully picture themselves at the point of success, experiencing success. Since they think it can't happen, they don't try. The truth is, you can't know for sure about anything unless you follow the steps necessary to reach a goal. You can dream big and reach for the stars. Trying is more important in most circles than actually making it. Chances are that if you really try, you will make it after all.

Goal setting is imperative if you want to truly see all your dreams and visions come to fruition. It doesn't matter if it's business-oriented or personal; setting a realistic and achievable goal and then working toward realizing that goal on a daily basis does work. You just have to do the work.

Once you experience success, you will be able to look back and realize that you achieve all success pretty much the same way. You set a goal, follow through on the tasks needed to be done for achieving results, keep an open mind, learn from others, track your successes and learn from your failures. It's the same thing, over and over again. And it works.

If you want to create a pattern of success in your life, you can start now by learning the secret that successful people know. Successful people are only special because they are doers who follow through. They are not smarter than others; in fact, it is entirely possible you are smarter on paper than they are. You just don't follow through.

Start at the top and learn how to craft the best goals for yourself. Know that your goal is something that can be accomplished and know that the goal is measurable before you finish writing it. People who achieve are doers. If you want to get something done, schedule it, no matter how silly it might seem to you. If you put it on a schedule at a particular time, and not just on a generic to-do list, you'll be more likely to get it done.

Automate the Mundane

There are a lot of things that need to be done but that can easily escalate into busy work. This doesn't get you closer to a goal. Bookkeeping, for instance, is something that can be accomplished today, and with the right software, almost automatically. You can schedule payments to happen automatically, and you can also use software that enters everything for you in the ledger. Freeing up time to focus on your scheduled activities that must be done to achieve the goal is a more productive use of time.

Sidebar

Busyness happens when we react to what's in front of us without stopping to consider if it matters or not. We get caught up in the urgency of the moment. Soon it becomes a habit, and before we know it, we end up busy. We become trapped in the urgency. Managers fall into the busyness habit when they allow weeks and months to drift by, drifting from activity to activity without stopping to consider if what they're doing is making any difference.

End Sidebar

Get Outside Expert Help

Being a success doesn't mean you have to do everything yourself. You're not on your own. The best scientists, professors, doctors, lawyers, and CEOs have assistants who help them look great. You too can hire outside help and contractors to help you do the tasks needed to reach your goals.

Stop reinventing the wheel! In most cases, someone has already done it before you. Someone has already worked out the kinks and devised a plan of action that will work for you too, with hardly any tweaks. Learn from other people's mistakes and realize that you can gain valuable information from what others are already doing.

Never Stop Learning

They say it takes ten thousand hours of reading about a topic to become an expert on any subject. Keep this in mind as you look toward your future and set your goals. If you want to be an expert, you'll need to start building up those ten thousand hours. Even if you know nothing about a topic today, you can be an expert in just ten thousand hours.

Know Your Core Values

As you set goals to create a pattern of success, it's imperative that you know what your core values are in terms of your family, personal, financial and physical life. Everyone has different areas they need to work on more than others. You need to know what your weak areas are so you can set realistic goals that you want to meet.

Track, Assess, Repeat

As they say, nothing is ever done without the paperwork. Well, that includes creating a pattern of success. Only by setting goals, then tracking and assessing the results of the goals, and then repeating what works, will you create a pattern of success.

Creating a pattern of success requires knowledge of goal setting, and goal achieving, and an in-depth knowledge of yourself. Starting today, you can gain that knowledge and create a real pattern of success in your life. One of the biggest mistakes people make when seeking to achieve a goal is to wait for inspiration and motivation. Imagine if everyone on this planet waited for motivation to get work done. Productivity would drop to nothing, and our economy would collapse. Since productivity has improved over the years, it's not likely that it has much of anything to do with real motivation other than people doing the things they have to do in order to achieve a goal.

How sad is it that in some cases people fail at so many things simply by ignoring the fact that motivation isn't really necessary; only doing is necessary. They sit around waiting for inspiration to come, wondering why everyone else is doing better than them. They're waiting for some spark of motivation that will never arrive. You can avoid this issue by realizing the truth.

Motivation Doesn't Exist

You've probably heard the myth of the starving artist who can't paint, or the writer with writer's block. It's interesting that these creative professions have the same myth, like weight loss, that some secret motivation has to come to achieve success. Some mysterious spark of inspiration will get you off your bottom and make you do what you need to get done. Nothing could be further from the truth.

Doing, Not Thinking, Gets Results

Time and again, the people who are truly successful in their own lifetimes, are not people who wait for a spark. They are people who get up out of bed every single day, rain or shine, and do things that lead to an end result of success. The successful painter paints every single day, and if they hate marketing, they hire someone to do that for them. The successful writer writes, the successful doctor doctors. If you want to be successful at something, do it. Live it. You will succeed.

Experience Success

Set some smaller goals so that you can feel what success is like. If you've never once stuck to anything, you can't know what success feels like; therefore, you have nothing to push you forward. People who experience success like to experience it again, and the more success you experience, the more you're going to realize that you can achieve success. It's self-fulfilling.

Repeat Everything

Finally, keep doing it over and over again. With anything you want to achieve, set the goal, track your success, and do something every single day toward achieving that goal. Again and again. It's really that simple. Motivation is a figment of the imagination, and not something that most people have. Most people get up in the morning by hitting the snooze button a few times, and most people do not feel especially happy about doing certain things. What they feel happy about is the end result, the deliverable. Place your focus there and you will not need any motivation because you will be successful.

Chapter 7
Do the Next Right Thing

Now that you've created your list of goals, this chapter shows you how to do what's necessary to achieve them. You should now be convinced that where you start your business venture is in your mind (because it is). It starts with a thought, and that thought leads to more thoughts. Taking that cultivated thought and putting pen to paper makes it a clear and concise vision statement.

What comes next is action. From your vision statement, you have created a good set of goals with timelines. Everyone's path will be different, but here are a couple stories of what happened next for our apartment business and our hot sauce business.

Sidebar

I have read and studied much of what Alan C. Walter has written, and he says, "Our thoughts create and predetermine the life we live, the environment we live in, our careers, the quality of relationships we engage in, the levels of power, wealth and happiness we are willing to experience or can have for ourselves or others."

End Sidebar

I had been working for a larger apartment developer for a few years, and I had grown restless. I started to think more and more about rolling the dice, but this time, my intention was set on creating wealth. I read book after book, and I formulated a plan. I envisioned a business where we developed, built, and sold condo units over retail space in an urban setting. The plan was to sell the condos and make enough profit to pay for the retail space and keep the retail for long-term cash flow.

Part of my daily morning meditation included "seeing it", meaning seeing the vacant lot, seeing a signed purchase agreement for the deal, seeing the construction workers building the project, seeing a finished building with people occupying the space. A few minutes each day is all it takes for the manifestation process to start to take hold. The universe delivers on what we think about, and as I placed emotion behind these thoughts, "things" started to appear. Suddenly, the floor started to move. This sensation would become more and more familiar as my dreams started to manifest.

Sidebar

Wayne Dyer describes manifestation: "There is a level of awareness available to you that you are probably unfamiliar with. It extends upwards and transcends the ordinary level of consciousness that you're most accustomed to. At this higher plane of existence, which you can access at will, the fulfillment of wishes is not only probable — it's guaranteed."

End Sidebar

I was having coffee at one of my favorite spots in our small town, just outside of Detroit, a quaint little bohemian place. While sipping on my coffee, I looked across the street and saw a for sale sign on a vacant lot, right in the middle of town. Holy smokes, could this be real? My head began to fill with negative chatter like, 'for sure it would be out of our price range', or 'why would the developer be selling it?' and so on.

I had never purchased a commercial property before, but one thing I learned from my years at my existing employer was whenever he would discuss developing a piece of property with any of the on-staff developers, his very first question was, "Do we have land control?" This meant, did we have the parcel tied up under contract? If the answer was no, that was the end of the conversation. You see, my employer learned from his vast experience in building and developing apartments (over 50,000 at the time), that without land control, it was just speculation, but if you had the piece of property tied up, your plans and conversation could actually go to the next level. Perhaps the larger point here is that there is such a significant difference in who you should listen to and intake advice from. Stick with people that have done what you want to do, and follow your intuition.

So, here was my first signpost that we talked about in the earlier chapter, right smack in front of me. When I looked across the street that winter afternoon, I saw my first-floor retail building with condo units above rising up from that vacant lot. Except my mental picture, and subsequently my vision statement, had underground parking under the retail space—that would never work on this flat lot. Except, as I walked across the street, I realized there was an alley behind this parcel, and the parcel was elevated ten to twelve feet above the alley, making this parcel a perfect fit! Holy cow, here it was right in front of me!

What unfolded next moved fast and furious. I created a one-page, simple letter of intent, which was accepted and led to a purchase agreement. That's great news, right? Except I had a full-time job and no formal plans or specifications for this development. Plus, the biggest thing I didn't have was money.

I had seven days to get enough capital together to get to the title company to hold in escrow. I went out on a limb and called in a couple of professional favors with an architect firm we had been working with. I needed a picture, a real color picture of what we might build. I was able to sell my idea and negotiate a very low price for a quick set of renderings that I could use to make a pitch to potential partners for this deal.

Don't ever be afraid to get creative, and to ask. In this instance, I was able to negotiate one price for these drawings if the project went through, and another, much, much lower price if the deal got nixed. The larger point here is that your relationships are key, and so very important.

Two things occurred here. First, had I been forced to pay full price for these drawings, the deal would have crashed before I ever presented it to anyone, but this architect was willing to take a chance on me. Second, you have to ask for things, even when it may be uncomfortable. Be open to a "no" and figure out a workaround. Not only did we get the drawings we needed at a significantly reduced rate, I got them in only two days from a firm that has a four to six-month backlog! I had seven days to find an equity partner, and I burnt two of those days selling the idea to the architect, and then two more with getting the drawing sketches done.

So, on day six, I pitched the deal to two investors that I knew, and who knew me. They loved it and said yes. The next day, day seven, they funded the required escrow payment with the title company, and we were in business. We went on to successfully develop the parcel. Remember the previous point about how work fills the allowable time space? I had seven days to figure this out, and we did. It happened, not because I was a genius, or lucky, or any of the other things folks yammer about, but mostly because I had a very clear intent, and when the world started to align with that intent, I acted. This became a common occurrence that happened over and over. Had it happened just once, I could easily side with the naysayers and agree that luck played a big part, but when something becomes a pattern, something much larger is in play.

When it comes to your business, you need to be as innovative, productive, and forward-moving as possible. There are many tools that you can utilize to maximize your creativity. Your stories will be different, but the process and the universal laws are the same.

Mind mapping is a way of brainstorming on paper. It is an extremely beneficial visual tool that stimulates creative thinking, thus preparing you to organize, evaluate, and analyze the data you create for your business ideas. It is sort of like brainstorming with yourself on paper.

To begin mind mapping, place a key word in the center of the paper that is a sort of the main character or central theme. Next, branch out ideas from that internal word and continue to branch out new words in a circle around that original word or theme.

The mind mapping system is similar to choosing a theme and several sub themes or topics and subtopics. The more you extend the circles and branch them out, the more creative you will become. Mind mapping is similar to choosing a niche and then a sub-niche and then another sub-niche within a sub-niche.

Benefits of Mind Mapping

Mind mapping offers several benefits. For one, mind mapping is a visual tool. It helps you organize information and create new concepts and themes while stretching your imagination. It also offers the possibility of analyzing and visualizing ideas on paper in a new and creative fashion.

Mind mapping is an excellent tool to evaluate the strengths of your company or business. By placing several key themes on paper, you can visually pinpoint your company's strengths. From there, you can gain momentum by brainstorming creative and innovative ideas to enhance and maximize those strengths.

Mind mapping is also useful in examining weaknesses. Weak areas are highlighted when using mind mapping. This is useful because sometimes a discussion about weaknesses does not produce any tangible results for improvement; however, using mind mapping creates a visual board that reveals where weaknesses lie.

If you want to explore opportunities that you can take advantage of, mind mapping is an excellent tool. If you have one or two tried and true ideas for success, you can create sub-categories and sub-topics for those opportunities. This, in turn, will create even bigger and more advantageous opportunities. If your company or business has the potential for external threats, using a mind map will clearly hone in on those threats and spotlight them. This is beneficial because you can now see where you need to put your attention to ward off potential outside threats in the future. Mind mapping is a very useful tool for assessing your strengths, weaknesses, opportunities, and threats.

Part of the challenge is figuring out what to do next. Business is a series of next steps. Alcoholics Anonymous (AA) has a great saying for those who have lost their way: "Do the next right thing." You won't find your next right thing in a book or in an instruction manual; you need to figure it out. Part of that comes from past experience. In the book *Outliers*, author Malcolm Gladwell says that it takes roughly ten thousand hours of practice to achieve mastery in a field. One approach is that you could choose a field and practice for 10,000 hours. If you are currently working in your target profession, forty hours per week over five years would give you ten thousand hours.

Or… we can look at the question in reverse. Where have you already logged 10,000 hours of practice? What is it that you do really well? What tasks do you perform so well that people ask, "How did you do that?" Sometimes, when we fall in love with practice, we don't even recognize it! If you're working at a company, what does your company do better than anybody else? Can you leverage your past experience as part of your 10,000 hours? How do you create an environment that gives you the opportunity to practice?

Sidebar

Champion: noun. One who makes their dreams and intentions an actuality by demonstrating mastery, competence, creativity, responsibility, ownership, and control over a specific area, endeavor, or subject.

End Sidebar

Since the creation of the internet and social media, hundreds of thousands of businesses have emerged. Of course, you want your business to stand out head and shoulders above the rest, but how do you achieve that goal? There are several ways to make your business stand apart from the competition.

Evaluate What You Have

It is often very easy to compare your company to others. The tendency may be to think that they do something better than you; however, it is most important to start from within. Evaluating your own company is the place to begin. Look in the mirror first. Take a good long look at where you have been static in your own company. Has your company become stale and outdated? Is there room for something new and innovative? Can you improve a product or service?

What can you reuse? Is there a sales letter that you can re-circulate or a product that you can enhance in order to gain new clients and customers? What needs recreating? Is there an area of your business, such as reorganizing one of your departments, that needs attention? Perhaps management and assistant management need to put better communication policies and procedures into place. Does your product or service live up to today's standards? Actually look and see if your product or service lives up today's standards. Once you have evaluated this, take a look and see if your product or service is trending according to today's standards.

Where do you stand with social media? If your website does not incorporate social media, then it is time to include this all-important aspect into your business. Many times, a customer will immediately leave a web page if he or she does not see social media buttons. How can you reach more clients? Investigate how you can reach more clients. Perhaps you need to set up a Facebook fan page if you do not already have one in place. Check to see if you are responding to comments that visitors leave on your webpage if you have one. Engaging with clients is a sure-fire way to bring them closer to you rather than alienating them. Reach out to other businesses and blogs to create a sharing opportunity on each other's web sites through guest blogging or blog rolls. Today, business is extremely fast-paced and moves at a rapid speed through change. Keeping up with those changes is the only way to stay ahead of the competition.

Competing for Shelf Space

In 2008, the real estate business in Detroit was not much fun. We had started a digital marketing and branding company a few years before Urbane Media. We found ourselves doing more marketing projects and less real estate development as the Great Recession nestled in. We were doing the social outreach and marketing for a local TV show that featured different restaurants and chefs each week.

It was a cool, local show, but it failed to find suitable funding the second year.

The lead character, Chef Tom, and I became friends, and he started hanging around our office. We spent some time bantering about this and that, trying to figure out a cool food business to get into. We ultimately landed on a hot sauce company. We tested Tom's hot sauce recipe and people loved it.

Six months later, we were licensed, and bottles of hot sauce were rolling out of our small-production commercial kitchen. The only trouble was, you have to sell a boatload of hot sauce just to break even. Although we were able to score some pretty big accounts and get into several retail stores early on, we were far off the mark of achieving enough production to make things work. We needed to figure out how to sell more hot sauce, and fast, as we had limited capital.

It seemed like we had two choices: 1) Increase the number of retail stores that sold our product, or 2) Figure out how to increase the amount of product sold per store. We leveraged several relationships, and that landed us in a lot of stores. So, we continued on that path; however, we decided to double down on increasing our sales yield per store. The problem was, that even with a really cool graphic on our bottle label, our product got lost in a sea of other hot sauce bottles.

Get Creative

We went to the hardware store and picked up fifty galvanized buckets. Then we had a local carpenter fabricate inserts that allowed us to stock two dozen bottles inside the bucket in a circle pattern. With this configuration, the hot sauce bottles stood up above the top of the bucket so the bottles were very visible, and the inner circle stacked higher. We had local art students paint the buckets, consistent with our branding.

The finished product was really cool, and the cost to create it was really low. The grocery store managers loved the bucket look with the hot sauce product inside it, and most of the stores allowed us to place the bucket on top of the meat counter. Our hot sauce was on the shelves with the other hot sauces, but now we were also on the meat counter, all by ourselves. The additional exposure helped us double our sales yield per store, and we were on our way to solving our problem.

While increasing our exposure by being on the meat counter and hot sauce aisle helped, we still needed to do more. We decided to further increase our sales yield, so we doubled down again on the sales per store. This time, we decided to target two to three restaurants around each retail store. We offered each of the restaurants free hot sauce for their tables. In exchange, we asked each restaurant to create a menu item that featured our hot sauce, and they had to keep our hot sauce on each of the tables. The cost averaged less than one to two cases per month. So, for less than fifty bucks a month per restaurant, we started to gain significant product exposure. Our sales per store soared!

An Entrepreneurial Mindset

In thinking about starting your own business, "stuff" will get in your way. There are several ways to tell if you have an entrepreneurial mindset. Moreover, there are just as many ways to clear the road to becoming an entrepreneur.

Consider these personality traits:

- ★ Leadership qualities
- ★ Creative thinking
- ★ A feeling that there is something more than what you are doing in your current job
- ★ Innovative ideas

If you show any or all of these qualities, you could very well be on your way to owning your own business because you do, in fact, have that entrepreneurial spirit. Going from the nine-to-five grind to the entrepreneurial spirit may not be the easiest path, but it is something you can achieve. However, there are several steps you need to take before forging head-first into business ownership.

Getting clear on what it is you want to achieve is an integral first step. It is not as simple as coming up with an idea and writing it down. You have to write down your goals, but even more importantly, you have to break them down. Being specific is not an option; it is mandatory. You need to have clear, specific goals when it comes to starting a new business.

Sometimes, in order to create something new, we need to let go of something old. In order to clear the path to creating a new business, something else will have to fall by the wayside. Your home may need to be a little cluttered or less clean. You may have to let go of a favorite sport or activity for a while, but it is well worth it in the end. Keeping your day job is important until you are financially secure in your new business endeavor. It may be a difficult road to travel, but having an entrepreneurial mindset is a gift. Once you open it, you will be happy that you did.

Chapter 8
Building A Brand on a Budget

One of the things that was important to me when we started our boutique apartment business was to create two things out of one for our new venture. First, I wanted to develop great cash flowing apartment communities that we could sell some day. Second, I wanted to create a management company to manage the apartment communities that also had value as a business that we could sell some day. One of the odd things that struck me about apartment operators is that they do not brand their product or properties, and while there are a few that do, most do not. A medium sized apartment operator may own and manage 8,000 units, which could be 35 to 40 apartment communities, and they might all be named something different. That just doesn't make any sense. Can you imagine Starbucks going by a different name in every city?

Sidebar

My good friend and fellow apartment maniac, Mike Brewer, describes GoogleJuice. "GoogleJuice is the ethereal substance which flows between web pages via their hyperlinks (in both directions!). Pages with lots of links to them acquire much GoogleJuice. Pages which link to highly juicy pages acquire some reflected GoogleJuice (do they? who says?). The level of GoogleJuice in a page thus reflects how well connected it is, and thus, in our world where links are content, how good it is (well, sort of). Google uses the term 'PageRank' in-house to mean the score that they give to each web page."

End Sidebar

While branding makes sense for a variety of reasons, Google loves, loves, loves reputation and similarity, as it significantly increases Google Juice. Conceivably, almost 85% of online users are starting their search for YOU and YOUR product on Google. Shouldn't your first question be, "Where does my brand show up on Google?" You need to know. The good news is, it is pretty darned easy to figure out, and you don't need your marketing director, your marketing agency or studio to give you some convoluted report. In our case, just Google 'Apartments (your city).' It is just that simple. You either place somewhere on page one of the Google Search or you don't. That's where the rubber meets the road.

Stop Accepting Excuses

I preface this first with, there are clearly some great marketing studios and PR firms, and they can add significant value; however, I, for one, have never really been able to separate out the BS when talking with marketing folks. Business folks have said forever, "I know that 50% of my marketing is working, I just don't know which half."

Well, your form of measure has never been easier. Just Google "Apartments (Your City)" or measure your brand awareness by Googling your company name. If you don't show up on page one, number one through five or six, you have work to do. If you Google your brand or company name and you do not DOMINATE the first few pages, then you don't have a brand, at least not one that anyone recognizes. If your staff, your marketing agency or your PR firm gives you guff about why you aren't on page one in a Google search, you might want to tell them to stop making excuses and deliver results.

Getting your branding right is really a big deal; it behooves you to spend some time on it. Marketing pundits love to confuse the issue of branding with logos, taglines, and an array of other propaganda. To me, branding is simply how we behave in our business. For instance, one of the ways we have distinguished the branding with our apartment management company is with our dress code, or lack thereof. We don't have one; in fact, we encourage flip flops in the summer months. That is how we behave, while other property management companies "suit up". While that is okay, what isn't okay is assuming that suiting up makes you more professional; it doesn't. Or that suiting up means your product is of higher quality; it doesn't. Or that suiting up means your product is luxury; it doesn't.

When we first started our Urbane brand, we struggled with what and who we were. Some of our staff thought we were luxury. Our staff equated our higher-than-normal rent per square foot and higher rent per unit than most of our competitors in southeast Michigan (sometimes being two to three times higher), to mean that we were a luxury brand. Except we weren't. In fact, we're far from it.

We wore flip flops on the leasing floor, all the while charging double or triple in rent what the guy across the street charged. In short, our staff equated high prices with luxury. Once we figured out what we weren't, it made it easier to figure out what we were. To use a car analogy, we were not a Mercedes, rather more of a Mini Cooper. Based on your brand, take some time to evaluate what will engage and delight your customer.

Many will tell you that an integrated approach to your marketing campaign is clearly the best approach. We have bucked that trend to prove a point that we got our boutique apartment management company, Urbane Apartments, to page one, number one, on a Google Search for 'apartments our city'. We were able to do that absent any paid advertising; no paid print ads and no paid internet ads. We did this only to show the power of creating resident evangelists and organic growth. Coming up high on a Google search, and getting the direct click to your website from the prospect is of significant value.

Here is the article that Jason Ankeny wrote about Urbane and our marketing and branding in Entrepreneur Magazine on April 13, 2010...

Chances are that anyone seeking a place to live in and around the trendy Detroit suburb of Royal Oak, Mich., eventually will come across property investment and management company Urbane Apartments. In fact, type "apartments Royal Oak" into the Google search toolbar, and the first result that pops up is the Urbane website—a destination highlighted by photos of the firm's modern, inviting rental units and the young urban professionals who occupy them.

With 16 apartment communities spanning across Royal Oak, Urbane has emerged as one of the region's fastest-growing property management companies. But the virtual prominence of its brand has little to do with its real-world scope. Credit instead, founder Eric Brown's decision to extend the firm's message into the social media realm—a move that not only slashed spending on paid property listings, but also afforded Urbane the tools to more accurately communicate the contemporary lifestyle experience so integral to its business.

"When I first announced to our staff that we were going to have a MySpace account, they looked at me like I was crazy," Brown recalls. "They said, 'We can't do that. Whenever we drop the ball, our tenants are going to write bad things about us.' I said, 'They may, and we will work to make those things right.' By reaching out and addressing those complaints, those residents became Urbane evangelists and started writing positive things about us. There's no way we could have the reach we have without hooking into the customer base we have.

Urbane Apartments now boasts a resident-penned blog touting favorite Royal Oak destinations, a social networking site exclusive to tenants (dubbed the Urbane Lobby) and active YouTube, Facebook and Twitter profiles. With each new post, photo, video and tweet, the company builds and nurtures its brand at no cost while fostering the hip, forward-thinking image its target demographic finds irresistible. According to Brown, in October 2008 about 100 people were visiting the Urbane blog each month. By the following spring, traffic grew to 4,500 visitors per month, and the number now tops 16,000 per month. Those metrics are even more impressive given that Urbane offers only about 300 rental units in all.

Urbane Apartments is the quintessential example of a small business that has maximized the possibilities of social media to champion its brand online, eschewing conventional advertising and search engine optimization solutions in favor of word-of-mouth buzz. Thanks to social networking, do-it-yourself website creation software and related tools, it's never been easier or cheaper to establish a beachhead online. Of course, the same alternatives are available to your competitors, meaning it's also tougher than ever to earn virtual visibility. That's where small businesses must get creative.

"The average small business doesn't need to worry so much about SEO or spending money on a web consultant. If they're out there and relevant to their audience, that's as much search engine optimization as they need," says Mike Whaling, president of 30 Lines, an online branding consultancy in Columbus, Ohio. "There are plenty of opportunities to build a strong brand on a small budget."

Regardless of how the message is articulated and distributed, the core mission of branding remains the same: communicating to customers who you are, what you do and how you do it. The web is the simplest, most direct channel to convey that information.

"Every company should have an online presence, and the cost of developing a site has come down to relative pennies," says Craig Reiss, founder of retail web developer Reiss Media in Cos Cob, Connecticut. "Organic search can still drive traffic. People go online looking for [a firm's service or product], and all you have to do is get found. It doesn't matter if you're a *single retailer and can't afford the time or have the expertise to drive traffic. Most people are just looking for directions to your store anyway."*

"Websites serve different purposes for different companies," says Nicholas Chilenko, principal of web design and internet marketing firm Nicholas Creative in East Lansing, Mich. Sometimes the goal is generating new business, sometimes it's about relaying messages to clients, and other times it's defining or even redefining the firm's image. "If someone wants to find out more information about you, they go to your website. It's the convergence of all your marketing messages," Chilenko says. "It's easy to create an identity because it's virtual."

"The challenge is getting that identity across in quick, broad strokes," says Mary van de Wiel, CEO of branding and communication design consultancy, Zing Your Brand, in Brooklyn. N.Y. According to her, businesses have just moments to succinctly communicate their purpose and value to consumers before they click away for good.

"You've got to be bold, you've got to be provocative, and you've got to be daring. Create a language and vocabulary that allows people to get that," Van de Wiel says. "Branding is what sets you apart—it's a natural magnet. If people come to your site, they need to say, 'Yes—this is who can answer my problem.' If you make a bad impression in the first five seconds, you're toast."

The most essential component of successful online branding is the human element, she says. "People are craving a story. They want to know something about who they're buying from, and they feel like they need to like and trust you," she explains. "You've got to shout what it is that makes you special and makes you different. Our personalities are what drive our brands. Look at Richard Branson—his personality is embedded in all of the Virgin brands. You need to put a face on your business."

Perhaps no tool is more effective at putting a human face on a firm than social media—and no tool is less expensive, either. In addition to utilizing social networking sites such as Facebook and Twitter, 30 Lines' Whaling recommends that small businesses introduce their own blogs as a means to pass along content that underscores the company's knowledge and expertise, with an emphasis on local information that directly affects customers. For example, an accountant might post about changes to city or state taxes that are likely to affect his clients, positively or negatively.

"Make sure you're regularly adding fresh content," Whaling advises. "Not only are you providing value, you're also adding pages to your website—that's more pages for search engines to index, and more opportunities for customers to find you."

"All businesses have information to share, regardless of vertical," he adds. *"Not enough companies take advantage of the opportunity to tell a story that's bigger than the company itself. There's always a story you can tell. Maybe your merchandise is made from local products or from sustainable materials. You've got to find that unique angle."*

For Urbane Apartments' Brown, the bigger story is the world that surrounds his properties. "At the end of the day, I'm not sure folks really care about apartment features. What they really want to know is what's going on nearby, like where is the best corner bar and the best place for sushi," he says. "Our blog focuses on everything about the local neighborhood—it's all about new bars and restaurants. And our website traffic is off the charts."

Social media outreach also lets businesses keep tabs on their online reputations and interact directly with fans and foes alike. According to Brown, Urbane Apartments closely monitors tenant reviews and feedback across multiple websites and is quick to respond to any criticism.

"A lot of folks want to ignore the ratings and review sites, which is a huge mistake. There's no hiding from that," Brown says. "If you're getting a bad review, you need to fix it and think about how to encourage good reviews. No longer does the general public believe in ads—they believe in what is said on Facebook."

Brown is applying to his own consulting business the lessons he's learned from building Urbane Apartments' online brand. Under the Urbane Way umbrella, he works with small businesses looking to pursue digital marketing opportunities. In late 2009, Brown also joined real estate information content provider Network Communications as a social media strategist. He practices what he preaches: Urbane Apartments dropped all print advertising and premium online promotions years ago, and Brown isn't looking back.

"Internet marketing is what enabled us to compete on a level playing field," Brown maintains. "I'm not suggesting print advertising is dead, but sometimes there's no money for that. There are certainly lots of pay-per-click programs, but how many times do you click on ads on Google? Most people never do that. But you can still build your brand organically. Wherever we can expand our digital footprint, we will do it."

Branded for life: Boosting your online image

Although experts agree that an engaging online presence is a must for any business, a user-friendly website and compelling products and services aren't enough to distinguish your brand from the rest of the pack. "Getting your brand out there and setting yourself apart should be easy, but it's not," says Mary van de Wiel, CEO of branding and communication design consultancy, Zing Your Brand. "You've got to be fearless, and you've got to live out loud—make yourself unmistakably unforgettable."

Here are some suggestions for making it happen:

Establish an identity. "If you can't work out what the unforgettable, differentiating spark is, you're a dead brand walking," Van de Wiel says. "It's a matter of working out what you want to do and working out the attitude of your brand. Your brand has a behavior and a tone. Brands like to show off and have fun. It wants to come out."

Be easy to find. "You want to make sure you're not invisible to search engines—that's why some people avoid all-Flash websites," says Mike Whaling, president of online branding consultancy 30 Lines. "Make sure you're represented in all the local directories. Go to GetListed.org, type in your business name and see where you come up on searches."

Steal good ideas and make them your own. "It's important to create a look and feel that represents your business in the best way, but not everyone has a design aesthetic, so you might need a little bit of help along the way," Van de Wiel says. "I recommend that people look around and see what speaks to them. If you can identify that, then track down the person who worked on that website. But be accountable, give the designer some benchmarks, and be clear about how you want to express your business."

Watch for opportunities. "Lots of people miss the boat in terms of call-to-action. Once you get people to your website, it's not always clear what you want them to do," says Nicholas Chilenko, principal of web design firm Nicholas Creative. "Make sure there's a clear path of motion through the site. The goal is to get customers to convert. Insert subtle cues throughout the copy and give them some incentive to make that initial contact."

Remember other marketing channels. "Don't forget about basic digital tools—e-mail marketing still works," Whaling says. "E-mail can feature posts from your blog; repurpose content you're using elsewhere. Also, leverage your offline promotions to complement what you're doing online. For example, list your Yelp page on your business card and encourage customers to go there to let you know how you're doing."

Chapter 9
Hitting the Wall

I cringe when I hear consultants say on social media, "fail faster." That's pretty bad advice, never strive to fail faster. To be clear, with your business, you can afford to fail in exact proportion to your available capital, and/or your ability to create credit with vendors, which sometimes happens before we know it. Mistakes are expensive. That is not to say it doesn't happen, but one should minimize errors as much as possible.

Perhaps the best advice is, if you have saved or set aside cash for your launch, double the cushion if you can. Businesses devour and consume cash. The cash just seems to evaporate. You can plan and plan and plan, and it just doesn't seem like there is enough cash. You make deals that you think you can cover, and then you can't. And then there is the shame, because the other thing we hear over and over from the armchair quarterbacks is, "You are only as good as your word," which IS true; however, what should you do when things just seem to keep coming apart? Maybe you resolve to work harder, work longer hours; just increase sales, that should do it.

Increasing sales with my construction business accelerated my demise, mostly because I didn't want to upset anyone. I worried more about what the customers thought of me, those with the purse strings, rather than just spilling the beans. Sales fixes all woes, right? Sort of. More sales is better than less, but sometimes, you sell and are high fiving everyone around you, super jazzed that you might just be able to cover the nut this month, except the new client doesn't pay, or they don't pay on time, which if you need the money, not paying on time is as painful as not paying.

It is not all gloom and doom, but expect the worst, because it does happen. And here is another thing; for us, it got tougher around year six or seven of our apartment management business. I had made so many mistakes, and I owed a lot of money to subcontractors and suppliers (they became the bank by default), and the economy was slowing. Something else also starts to invade you when the chips are down; your quality of decisions declines rapidly. In my case, I continued to channel wrong thinking.

I had an idea... What if we were to start doing our own in-house snow removal? Yes, that would be great! The apartment communities we managed would pay us timely, and we already had some built-in business. Off to Craigslist I went to buy a plow and truck. Within a few days we were set up to start plowing snow—bring it on, we were ready! And bring it on it did! That winter we had record snowfall, which, as you might guess, crushed us. Our truck broke down, and the snow began to pile up at our properties. And it got worse, as you might expect. With an avalanche of snowfall, every snow removal company was jammed busy, and our old contractor told us to take a hike for not using them in the beginning of the season. We were stuck, and so were our residents, no pun intended. We eventually found a contractor to do the work, but at a premium-plus price.

This escapade became a financial nightmare. We ended up paying the old contractor for cancelling their contract, even though they didn't plow any snow, and we paid the contractor who ended up cleaning up the mess three times what the normal costs would be. So, what was intended to be a 'save the day by doing something in-house' turned out to be a financial mess. Another costly mistake. Perhaps it looks and sounds like an easy one to have avoided; after all, it seemed like a great idea at that time.

Business continuity encompasses a loosely defined set of planning, preparatory, and related activities. They are intended to ensure that an organization's critical business functions will either continue to operate despite serious incidents or disasters that might otherwise have interrupted them or will be recovered to an operational state within a reasonably short period. As such, business continuity includes three key elements, and they are:

1. Resilience: critical business functions and the supporting infrastructure are designed and engineered in such a way that they are materially unaffected by most disruptions, for example through the use of redundancy and spare capacity.
2. Recovery: arrangements are made to recover or restore critical and less critical business functions that fail for some reason.
3. Contingency: the organization establishes a generalized capability and readiness to cope effectively with whatever major incidents and disasters occur, including those that were not, and perhaps could not have been, foreseen. Contingency preparations constitute a last-resort response if resilience and recovery arrangements should prove inadequate in practice.

In thinking about continuity in business, or as it is coined above, business continuity, I can't help but think about our own struggles. By that, I mean, what do we do in our business when things are not going right?

I was speaking at a conference in Tulsa, Oklahoma, and someone asked me for some examples of what went wrong along the way with our start-up business. Now heading into year fifteen, it was not really a start-up anymore. The short answer is, "plenty," except we rarely talk about that.

Maybe it's our ego or sometimes the pain and embarrassment of screwing up. There are certainly different shades of errors and mistakes, but at the core, business continuity is often described as 'just common sense'. It is about taking responsibility for your business and enabling it to stay on course, whatever storms it is forced to weather. It is about "keeping calm and carrying on"!

In reading some Essential Drucker this weekend, I came across this favorite quote: *"The truly important problems managers face do not come from technology or politics; they do not originate outside of management and enterprise. They are problems caused by the very success of management itself."*

So, therefore, thinking that we get better and better at business as time wears on, isn't exactly accurate. For sure, we eventually stop making rookie mistakes, but what about the problems caused by the very success of management itself that Drucker refers to? I gave a lot of thought to this as of late, as some of the problems we are working on at one level makes it seem as if we are tripping up at the basics; yet, overall, we have a highly profitable, successful company. Nonetheless, these problems are real, they do exist, and they need to be solved.

The less than flattering news is, why does it take so much effort to fix?

Business continuity may well be the answer, as it is about building and improving resilience in your business. It's about identifying your key products and services and the most urgent activities that underpin them and then, once that 'analysis' is complete, it is about devising plans and strategies that will enable you to continue your business operations and enable you to recover quickly and effectively from any type of disruption, whatever its size or cause. It gives you a solid framework to lean on in times of crisis and provides stability and security.

In the 1970s, the philosophers Samuel Gorovitz and Alasdair MacIntyre published a short essay on the nature of human fallibility. The question they sought to answer was, 'why we fail at what we set out to do in the world'. One reason, they observed, is "necessary fallibility"— some things we want to do are simply beyond our capacity. We are not omniscient or all-powerful. Even enhanced by technology, our physical and mental powers are limited. An example of this is the 36-percent increase between 2004 and 2007 in lawsuits against attorneys for legal mistakes—the most common being simple administrative errors, like missed calendar dates and clerical screw ups, as well as errors in applying the law. So, is it as easy as just creating checklists?

I am a checklist nut, and I do feel checklists create consistency. We recently had a senior employee leave our company, and while we hear all the time the value of our best employees, it becomes in-your-face evident when someone leaves who has been around for an extended period of time. Knowing this all to be true, I completely underestimated the productivity decrease and general chaos that followed when a decade-long employee left our company. What I became acutely aware of is just how vulnerable our business was, or is, without a continuity in business plan.

Sometimes, we cause our own crisis. It seemed like a great idea to move a high performing leasing person over to a sister property that needed some help, but we seldom stop to really think through the ramifications of cannibalization. There is always an energy dynamic in the workplace, a defined way they function as a group, yet we tend to not think of the interconnectedness as maybe being the core reason for the collective success. We repeat past history over and over by not accounting for dynamic collaboration. We wake up to the nonsense when occupancy falls like a rock. Most in our office will not agree, or even see the correlation that we caused the demise by not recognizing the inner connections of a successful working model. Perhaps it would be clearer if we removed one leg of a four-legged chair and we asked our executive management group to sit on it, and then convince them everything is okay.

The overarching point here is that many times our disruption of continuity in business is a cause and effect of our own internal irrational behavior and wrong thinking. Often, it's disguised as being the best choice, but many times it isn't, and we never really see our part in creating the dysfunction.

Most of our mistakes were avoidable, had we been more awake. That seems odd writing that now; however, one becomes numb to the pain. We dug such a deep hole with mistake after mistake, that we couldn't get out of business if we wanted to. There were numerous sleepless nights of worrying. We had hit the wall.

As I look back, I ask myself, would I do it again? For sure I would, but just a little sooner in life. I think that building a successful business, one with structure, meaning there are buildings, equipment, employees and so forth takes time, sometimes years, sometimes decades. Friends, I think the pain is inevitable, and many times we just aren't prepared. The phrase, "An entrepreneur is the only soul that would exchange a forty-hour week for an eighty-hour week just to be self-employed," rings true.

The dysfunction of our business in the first ten years or so was well masked. Urbane Underground, as we dubbed our office, was a strange sort of setup. It was in the basement of one of our urban apartment buildings, except part of the area was above ground. The entire south wall was windows, except you were looking at people's feet walking on the sidewalk. While it is a cool space, it is equally a bit strange, although a much-improved upgrade from where we started.

I would sit at my desk looking out the window at sidewalk pedestrians' feet, sometimes feeling like we were in a fishbowl, and wondering if they only knew how upside down we were. I say that because, from the outside looking in, we appeared to be pretty successful. We had acquired, rehabbed, and repositioned a dozen or so Urbane branded apartment communities that first decade. We had been recognized and written up by the New York Times, Harvard Business Review, Newsweek Magazine, and even a six-page spread in Entrepreneur Magazine. Yes, to the outside world, we were a success story; yet inside, the pain points were increasing to nearly unbearable proportions.

Part of the issue is, who do you talk to? In my case, I could talk to my wife, except that just made our already rocky homelife more uncomfortable. How could we be living in an apartment at our age? What were we going to retire on? Were we even going to be able to retire?

You see, I am a bit of a dreamer; perhaps all entrepreneurs are dreamers. That dreamer thing serves us well in the beginning but becomes a point of shame when things aren't going so well. In fact, it becomes part of your partner's ammunition. I shall never forget my dear wife's words to me late one night when she said, "Just how long do you intend to toil away at that business?" My answer of, "As long as it takes," didn't go over well, but that is the answer: as long as it takes. The point here is, be prepared for a journey of unexpected ups and downs.

Our attributes are a double-edged sword. Some of the things that propel us and create separation between us and them, with them being the competitor, can cause both failure or success. For me, I have never been all that afraid to spend money I didn't have. This seems a little strange to some people I know, but it happened frequently. I always assumed many start-up businesses operated in this fashion. Isn't that where the term "bootstrapping" came from?

Fortunately, I was able to push back the demons long enough to start to get some traction, by making a conscious effort to do the next right thing, day after day. An Army Ranger friend of mine said recently during a lunch meeting, "The map is not the ground." He explained that, even after studying an area, the landscape and a well-detailed plan always looks very different than it does on the map. Your business trek will be no different. A business plan is good, but be prepared for the twists and turns, some of which will make your head spin.

At some point, you just need to start making better choices and better decisions. Do the next right thing, as they say—and keep at it.

I had an email exchange with a multifamily executive who extended a nice compliment to us regarding our social marketing. She expressed that she may be looking for a marketing person with a similar "vibe". My response was, "I think social outreach and social marketing is more of a trained and managed process rather than a trait that a marketing hire may or may not have. That said, the "vibe" is more about culture, which can be more challenging to effect change. It occurred to me at that moment that what we were doing, day in and day out, was our culture, and although we had hit the wall, maybe even rammed it multiple times, we were creating a culture which would carry us to success. Years later, I would go on to work extensively with that multifamily executive to help reshape their culture, but first we needed to better understand our own and what was unfolding.

The Urbane leasing staff have no ensembles and there is no dress code. They are in jeans most days and wear flip flops all summer. We do not go on tours with prospects. We send prospects out on their own to tour our apartments. In our trek to enhance the concept of a centralized leasing center at Urbane, we developed a new way to tour apartments that we coined "GO SOLO". It works like this... The prospect meets at Urbane Underground first to go over their living space needs. For folks who have never experienced the Urbane Underground, it is pretty "interesting and entertaining" and sets the tone for a fun encounter. We LOVE pets at Urbane. There are no pet fees, no size restrictions and no breed restrictions.

The point here is that our "culture", the way in which we conduct business, the way in which we behave each day, is anything but industry norm, and that was setting us far, far apart and helping us break away from the pack of apartment commodities. It IS who we are, and it isn't for everyone. Social outreach and social marketing were just an extension of our day and what we do.

Company culture is important because it can make or break your company. Companies with an adaptive culture that is aligned to their business goals routinely outperform their competitors. Some studies report the difference at 200% or more. To achieve results like this for your organization, you have to figure out what your culture is, decide what it should be, and move everyone toward the desired culture.

Company cultures evolve and they change over time. As employees leave the company and replacements are hired, the company culture will change. If it is a strong culture, it may not change much. Since each new employee brings their own values and practices to the group, the culture will change, at least a little. As the company matures from a startup to a more established company, the company culture will change. As the environment in which the company operates (the laws, regulations, business climate, etc.) changes, the company culture will also change.

These changes may be positive, or they may not. The changes in company culture may be intended, but often they are unintended. They may be major changes or minor ones. The company culture will change, and it is important to be aware of the changes.

There are many ways to assess your company culture. There are consultants who will do it for you, for a fee. The easiest way to assess your company's culture is to look around. How do the employees act? What do they do? Look for common behaviors and visible symbols.

Listen. Listen to your employees, your suppliers, and your customers. Pay attention to what is written about your company, in print and online. This feedback will give you clues as to what your company's culture really is.

Before you can change the company culture, you have to decide what you want the company culture to look like in the future. Different companies in different industries will have different cultures. Imagine what kind of culture will work best for your organization in its desired future state. Review your mission, vision, and values and make sure the company culture you are designing supports them.

You need to align your company culture with your strategic goals if it isn't already aligned.

- Develop a specific action plan that can leverage the good things in your current culture and correct the unaligned areas.
- Brainstorm improvements in your formal policies and daily practices.
- Develop models of the desired actions and behaviors.
- Communicate the new culture to all employees and then
- over-communicate the new culture and its actions to everyone.

Only a company culture that is aligned with your goals, one that helps you anticipate and adapt to change, will help you achieve superior performance over the long run.

Chapter 10
Living the Dream

It is a fascinating revelation to one day realize that you are no longer dragging your knuckles on the ground. At first blush, you continue to hunker down, expecting the next wave to come thrashing at the dock... except it doesn't. As you take some time to reflect, you look at those knuckles, and the scars; the bumps and bruises have started to heal. It doesn't seem real, or even possible, and you are skittish, very skittish.

I was unsure what was happening, but things were different. We started to actually have enough available money each month to pay our bills, and our legacy debt had shrunk to a manageable number. While this was a much welcome relief, it was nonetheless a strange encounter. I was a bit unsure of myself. Could I be success resistant? Pinch myself. This is working. Holy cow!

Little by little, we had crawled out of the hole, and the view was pretty incredible. To be clear, we were not basking in the sun on a tropical beach, but our business was operating independently, and we had shrunk our expenses to such a point that we were able to start to accumulate cash, after building a much-needed reserve. The dumb mistakes seemed to dry up. I would like to say that this day was planned, and that we brilliantly navigated to this exact point, except we didn't, but somehow we had made it.

The spreadsheets listing available revenue and expenses were suddenly working. It occurred to me that the seemingly endless list of lawsuits and people wanting money, money, and more money had dried up. We started to have payroll and tax money for our staffing set aside a week in advance. That was a far cry from waking up in a cold sweat Thursday night, not knowing how we would cover payroll on Friday.

Another oddity was unfolding; I started to buy some silver and gold. First in small orders, but eventually, it would add up. I was actually investing in something, and watching it grow. I like silver and gold because, like real estate, I can hold it, look at it, feel it, and... cash it in should "something happen." It gave me comfort, and I wanted to increase that comfortable feeling.

What started as a small stream, passive income from cash flow distributions from the property performance was increasing each passing quarter. The lesson here is that things can change pretty fast, and with a compound effect. Not only was our business becoming profitable, the assets, meaning properties that we owned and managed, were starting to spin off nice cash on cash returns.

You see, the sole reason for starting the journey on that Sunday afternoon on the front porch was to create wealth, and to escape from the rat race as Robert Kiyosaki so explains over and over in the Rich Dad book series. Could this actually be happening?

About the same time that this was all coming to light, I received a couple of opportunities to speak again. I had done a fair amount of speaking nationally a few years back, but lost interest. Some of it seemed fake. Here I was, out there touting how our means and methods of digital marketing and branding were all that and a bag of chips, yet in reality, our business was ever so close to the rocks. The other thing that happened is that a handful of my multifamily peers put us in a cubby hole, saying that the grandiose ideas only worked for two reasons: 1) Our business was small, and the ideas would never scale and 2) I was hands on, and the ideas would never scale. Both were true for sure. We were small and I am a hands-on guy, but I was sure they would scale. Little did I know that I was about to find out.

It was a beautiful afternoon in July when I received two opportunities to speak in the same week. Being one to believe that there is no such thing as a coincidence, and these engagements were both paid gigs, and they were both in the midst of the preceding winter, it seemed like maybe I should sharpen up my PowerPoint slides and hit the speaking circuit again. So that's what I did. The following February landed me in San Francisco, presenting on digital marketing to apartment operators. On the second day of the conference, a young man approached me and said that his mom told him to look me up. I didn't recognize his company at first, but then I remembered a LinkedIn email from Lesley Brice, partner and president of MC Residential, several months back asking about our marketing vibe at Urbane Apartments. I had not responded.

We were having a particularly harsh winter in Detroit that year, and I alluded to that in a follow-up message to Lesley that I had met her son. An email dialog ensued that landed me in Scottsdale, Arizona two months later to start a significant digital marketing project for MC Companies; an experiment to see if these crazy Urbane ideas would actually work and scale over their 8,000-unit apartment portfolio. The fun was about to begin.

A year into the project, we just finished our first annual investor summit at MC Companies, and it was a really cool event. Over fifty of our investors from all over the world came together to meet and greet our MC Company's operations team. It caused me to reflect on what a ride it had been the last year in the wild west of Arizona, Texas, and Oklahoma apartment marketing of over 8,500 units in seven regions. Over that first last twelve-month period, we covered a bunch of ground, stubbed our toes a bit learning the nuances of scale, but we were pretty juiced up about where we are. Scaling these ideas was much tougher than I had anticipated. I had been used to being the boss and calling the shots for a long time. Suddenly, I found myself in a support role, with no staff—something that was very foreign to me.

Scaling new projects at a new company was by far and away the most challenging thing I had done to date in my career. Scaling is on my mind every day now. It is very clear to me why individuals don't stick their neck out on new projects, particularly game changing projects. It isn't the risk of failure; it is the passive aggressive ridicule and ongoing slamming from within that deters people from doing greater things. It shows up as a side joke in front of your boss, just enough to plant the doubt seed, or a kick in the gut when you are down on one knee gasping for air because you are trying to do two jobs; yours and the project you want to create.

I would guess this sounds a bit over dramatic, unless you have really tried to scale something of significance where you don't own the company.

Sidebar

Mike Brewer, great friend and fellow multifamily maniac, weighs in. "Scaling is an artisan's work that plays out over a very long bit of time. The muse is ever changing, the fringe ever unforgiving. The pursuit is to come full circle to where you began and to know it for the first time. The key to getting there is to serve the people that serve the cause and to build them into champions of life and charismatic all-stars of awesomeness. The rest fall prey to realizing their own underlying thoughts and opinions as the genius and courage of others."

End Sidebar

We are a society that loves parades, pep rallies, and celebrations. The same holds true in business. We love to set lofty goals and celebrate what we hope will become reality; however, we've not been willing to make the required commitment to change. Everybody talks a good game. Every company gives lip service to taking performance up a notch and being the best that they can be. We pick a theme for the next company meeting: Riding the Waves of Change! ... Dominate the Market! ... Total Customer Satisfaction! ... The Success Zone! ... The Power of One! ... The Power of the Team! ...

Businesses mistakenly assume that all employees want to be the best, but, more importantly, are willing to do what it takes in terms of commitment, change, and hard work to make it happen. ***This is a false and dangerous assumption.***

We were working on a new approach to our digital presence at MC Companies. Our first order of business was to ditch the rented websites and create a regional map-based apartment search. We believed that grouping our apartment communities by geographical region on a single site would help us with search and be useful to the prospects.

Our first site to launch was MCLifeTucson.com. We rebranded our social outreach as MC Life, with regional Facebook pages and centralized Pinterest, Flickr, Instagram, Yelp and Foursquare accounts. Our content focus was on lifestyle; all things hyper local; Eat Shop Play.

Early on with our Urbane Brand, much before we ever heard the phrase content marketing, we said, if we can create an online experience with enough value, then renting apartments is secondary, and now we have something special.

There are lots and lots of pieces to the puzzle. Achieving digital domination is not a single thing. It isn't just your website or your SEO strategy, or your Twitter followers, or your Facebook fans. It is an array of little things, all tied together, pulling in unison, both with online and offline tactics.

Your offline behavior greatly affects the outcome and result. One such piece is Go Solo Tours; it screams, "We are different," the minute the prospect walks in your door. Done right, you can increase your open for business by 40% without increasing leasing labor, thus allowing your leasing office to be open from 8:00 AM to 8:00 PM five days a week and 9:00 AM to 6:00 PM Saturday and Sunday. If you want to rent more apartments, be open for business longer hours. Closing up a leasing office before 8:00 PM during the week and not being open all day Saturday and Sunday is designed with the property management company in mind, not the leasing prospect.

A regional website allows deployment of centralized leasing leads. With one-off, stand-alone websites, the leasing traffic/leasing leads are directed to the community website that the prospect clicked on. However, with a regional website, leasing Leads are centralized, and the leasing staff has some influence on where to direct that leasing traffic. It also allows us to manage that traffic in a single funnel, as opposed to one-offs. The backbone of centralized leasing is that the prospect can view online unit availability.

We launched two MC Life lead-to-lease hubs in the first year: one in San Antonio, TX and the other in Tucson, AZ. The lead-to-lease hubs handle all inbound leasing leads and schedule all leasing tours for all MC residential communities. These centralized hubs manage all leasing traffic and our rental inventory.

Lead-to-lease hub is a fancy-pants name for a call center. Centralizing our inbound leasing leads increased our overall leasing traffic significantly. The typical leasing person at an apartment community has a zillion things to do, in addition to leasing apartments. Our call center's in-house staff's only objective is to convert leasing leads to appointments. This would prove to be a pivotal piece to the puzzle of success.

Our MC Life branding included reorganization of our social outreach marketing strategy to significantly grow our friends, fans and followers of our MC Life brand. We expanded to three full-time social media coordinators who create and curate content via images, video, and articles.

We also brought on a full-time social outreach coordinator to manage the MC Life partnership marketing initiatives and relationships and the MC Life event marketing in the seven regions in which we operate to establish relationships and negotiate agreements with key stakeholders as a media partner for select events and festivals in these regions. The position also helped promote the regional MC Life co-work spaces and establish a products list and collateral for advertising sales opportunities for MC Media, a company yet to be formed.

I am a big believer in writing things down. Blogging helped me better envision the future and organize my thoughts. I am also a huge fan of an Ann Arbor based business, Zingerman's Deli. One of their must-follow business practices is a vision statement, which we wrote about earlier. Below is the vision statement we created for MC Residential in early 2014. It outlined our ideas surrounding branded media before we started the project. It is interesting how close to par things have turned out.

Districts and Neighborhoods: *Visioning a Fresh Approach to Apartment Marketing*

Apartment community websites across the land are broken. Most are stagnant, with few updates in years. They have a low or no Google PageRank. Prospects cannot find a lost website. The "content management system" has failed. Apartment managers do not really know what to update regularly. Having a blog attached is a fragmented approach at best. Then there is Facebook and Twitter and YouTube and LinkedIn and Pinterest and Instagram. Who manages and creates the content—the property manager, leasing agent, or someone from corporate? Are there separate accounts for each apartment community? This mess needs to be fixed.

I am proposing a solution specifically for the mid-sized apartment operator like MC Companies, designed to replace the typical static apartment community website. This apartment marketing and leasing website will incorporate hyper-local articles and be everything local, similar to what Airbnb recently launched with <u>*Neighborhoods*</u>*. With a fully automated web-based lead to lease lead collection and tracking system woven into the fabric of the site as a seamless part of the user experience, effectively managing leasing leads is easy. Being fully automated is a key component. Too many leasing leads become lost sticky notes. Each component and touch point will be designed around the concept of enhancing the leasing experience. The site will sport strong and pleasing graphics, local photography, and video illustrating all things local via a variety of content mediums and reviews.*

The website framework will be "responsive" and adjust to any size screen, including mobile. The sites will be organized by geographical regions, referred to as "districts" with fresh, targeted lifestyle content on the neighborhoods in which we operate apartment communities. Think about everything hyper-local; restaurant and bar reviews, local music, art, and festivals. The content will be loaded with crisp images of local nightlife, shopping, dining, public transit and walkability.

The responsive website will incorporate a streamlined guest card and unit availability sheet, which auto-flow into a web-based lead to lease management system. The guest card will be simple and sleek and will capture first and last name, email and cell phone number only. The user's email and text number will automatically download into an email/text marketing program. The guest card will be prominently placed on the MC Community Facebook page and each digital asset, as appropriate, and all information will flow directly into the lead to lease system. The regional or district Facebook pages would mirror the brand images of the regional or district web pages.

One of the key points of organizing the apartment operator's affairs and digital assets regionally, by neighborhoods, is to steer away from single one-off apartment community Facebook pages, Twitter accounts, Pinterest accounts, YouTube and so forth. This creates an excellent opportunity to brand the property lifestyle. Every apartment community has a persona and a certain lifestyle. This new website will better convey that. The challenge of managing one-off social marketing at the community-by-community level does not scale. Content marketing, partnership marketing, and social outreach become much more effective and manageable by region.

Unit availability by region or by neighborhood will be incorporated and will be a centralized, real-time place for daily updates of unit availability. The unit availability will include unit photos, 3D floor plans, and videos cataloged by unit type and will be a clickable link that opens a window on the unit availability.

The website will be clean and simple. Less is more. Fill the space with great photography, local reviews, and all things hyper-local. Each page will have a clear call to action leading prospects into the sales funnel; however, this is an "opt-in" experience, meaning the prospect decides when the conversion process starts. We expect that prospects will stay on the site much longer and may visit several times before renting. The site will make every effort to "match" the prospect to a certain apartment community based on the property strengths and personality. Each apartment community will be assessed and categorized. Each apartment landing page will include the Walk Score widget and will expand a window with all things local. The site will include articles and reviews to coincide with these local neighborhood businesses that are in alignment with the apartment's brand and core targeted demographic.

Partnership marketing opportunities will be negotiated with these core businesses that make the match. These rich relationships provide excellent cross marketing opportunities. For instance, helping promote the local burger joint is an opportunity to give away something as a promotion from the burger joint on the apartment operator's Facebook page at no cost to the apartment operator. The site will automatically capture email address and text numbers with each guest card. Appropriate language will be embedded to allow the user to request future emails about neighborhood events, new business openings, festivals, and local news happenings. Regular email offerings would be processed to keep in touch with prospects and residents on all things local.

So, with the last paragraph, we came full circle. We organized ourselves to be our own branded media. We have created a tight-niche media company inside the confines of a real estate investment company. Our core service is to provide leasing leads, marketing and PR for the various MC Companies brands; MC Residential, MC Fitness, MC Life, MC House Mates, MC Overnight and After 55.

Our next task was to strip out all paid advertising from our apartment marketing strategy and drive down our marketing and advertising costs. We also planned to start selling advertising and apartment tours to other property management companies. These ideas were coming to life, and better yet, were working at scale!

As our MC Life branding project at MC Companies began to near the 24-month mark, we couldn't have been happier as to where we were. We successfully expanded our digital footprint and had two consecutive quarters under our belt with enough self-generated leasing leads to sustain acceptable occupancy at our 8,500-unit apartment portfolio.

Our apartment operations in the seven regions, across three states, were humming along nicely.

Here is the big news... We lowered our marketing and advertising costs by 96% to just under $75 per unit per year; down from $153 per unit per year in 2013. That represented over a $600,000 savings portfolio wide.

The MC Life 555 Partnership Marketing Program set the stage to fuel a solid advertising vertical for MC Media. With 30 businesses around each MC apartment community, we have over 1,200 eat/shop/play related businesses on our websites. These rich relationships provide excellent cross-marketing opportunities. We are seeing these types of partnership marketing opportunities unfold now. The next logical step is to integrate advertising revenue opportunities with these eat/shop/play partnerships we have created.

Apartment operations pose an interesting growth opportunity that may be mostly misunderstood. If operations are doing even an average job at operating the property, the enterprise cannot expand like other businesses. There are a finite number of units to rent each year. As leasing traffic starts to exceed rental inventory, most apartment operators back down paid advertising to create a balance to hold occupancy levels at or around 93% to 95%. They adjust rental rates in accordance with what the perceived competitor is doing. This is referred to as comp shops.

We believe that this is a flawed process. As paid advertising subsides and organic website traffic increases to yield more leasing traffic than inventory, rental rates rise with the tide. This is different due to the convergence of paid-owned-shared-earned (POSE) media, which is completely disrupting how marketers ... market.

Paid media is brand content enabled through payment (includes paid search, sponsored content, promotions, advertising, etc.); **owned media** is brand content published on a brand's channel (includes websites, social media channels, blogs, apps); **shared media** is consumer content enabled by a third party (includes organic search, forums, user-generated content, "likes" and retweets or comments, etc.); and **earned media** is consumer content enabled by a third party (media coverage, etc.).

As MC Media continues to leverage paid and owned media in order to scale, with the goal of amplification, spreading messages to connect with customers and leveraging POSE to drive effectiveness, achieve authenticity, cultivate ideas, and cut through the noise, MC Life will become prominent in geographical apartment search.

Branded media means that we become the advertiser. It works and is an extremely effective edge for lowering apartment marketing costs. The dirty little secret is that apartment marketing costs continue to decrease over time as you build your content arsenal. As our digital footprint expands year over year with creative, useful content, our SEO benefit expands accordingly. The average apartment operator's number of units to rent is static year over year and doesn't expand unless there is a lease up.

As long as apartment marketers continue to primarily spend their marketing budgets on ILS ads, they aren't very serious about ANY type of media marketing. Some have done paid search, but that is the extent of their media marketing. Paid search has mostly been ineffective. The irony is that if they were to pursue paid media, owned media, shared media or earned media, they would realize that their biggest competitor isn't the apartment community across the street; it is their ILS Partners. By and large the ILS's own the search market and they will outspend most apartment marketers. However, with diligence, the savvy apartment marketer can level things up with local content and partnership marketing, which fuels a well-oiled local search campaign.

Partnership marketing served as an excellent strategy to bridge the gap between starting our branded media campaign and garnishing enough website traffic to self-sustain enough leasing leads to keep our apartment communities full. Hitching our wagon to someone else's wagon, when appropriately aligned, is very effective.

Partnership marketing will help us get noticed, and when we get noticed by the national media, only good things happen. MC Media will serve as a media partner for local festivals and restaurant associations, as well as a sponsor of local events. As these relationships matured, late in 2016 and early in 2017, MC Media started to sell various advertising models. At a 20% penetration of the (950 to 1,100) MC Life eat/shop/play partnerships, selling ads, social media marketing, and cross marketing opportunities create approximately $1,500,000 of annualized advertising sales for MC Media, just by leveraging the existing contacts and relationships we have created.

As our lead to lease hubs mature and get better and better at farming leasing leads with increased yields in the form of apartment tours, and our website traffic continues to swell, we start to have more leasing traffic than available units. The next natural service for MC Media is to start to sell tours. We believe that we can sell apartment tours. Assuming the client apartment operator has confidence, we could supply them with enough leasing tours, we can actually lower their marketing and advertising expenses.

So, the crazy ideas did scale, and it was a fun experiment.

Now, what's next for Eric Brown?...

About Eric Brown

Eric Brown's background is rooted in the rental and real estate industries. He founded metro Detroit's Urbane Apartments in 2003, after serving as senior vice president for Village Green Companies, a Midwest apartment developer. He established a proven track record of effectively repositioning existing rental properties in a way that added value for investors while enhancing the resident experience. He also established The Urbane Way, a social media marketing and PR laboratory, where innovative marketing ideas are tested.

Made in the USA
Las Vegas, NV
21 July 2021